Series/Number 07-137

SPLINE REGRESSION MODELS

LAWRENCE C. MARSH
University of Notre Dame

DAVID R. CORMIER
Indiana University, Kokomo

SAGE PUBLICATIONS
International Educational and Professional Publisher
Thousand Oaks   London   New Delhi

For information:

Sage Publications, Inc.
2455 Teller Road
Thousand Oaks, California 91320
E-mail: order@sagepub.com

Sage Publications Ltd.
6 Bonhill Street
London EC2A 4PU
United Kingdom

Sage Publications India Pvt. Ltd.
M-32 Market
Greater Kailash I
New Delhi 110 048 India

Printed in the United States of America

Library of Congress Cataloging-in-Publication Data

Marsh, Lawrence.
　　Spline regression models / by Lawrence C. Marsh and David R. Cormier.
　　　　p.　cm. – (Quantitative applications in the social sciences;
　　07-137)
　　Includes bibliographical references and index.
　　ISBN 0-7619-2420-5
　　　　1. Social sciences–Statistical methods. 2. Regression analysis.
　　I. Cormier, David R.　II. Title.　III. Sage university papers series.　Quantitative applications in the social sciences; no. 07-137.
　　HA29 .M26127　　2001
　　300′.5′19536–dc21　　　　　　　　　　　　　　　　　　　2001019807

This book is printed on acid-free paper.

02　03　04　05　06　10　9　8　7　6　5　4　3　2　1

Acquiring Editor:	C. Deborah Laughton
Editorial Assistant:	Veronica Novak
Production Editor:	Denise Santoyo
Production Assistant:	Kathryn Journey
Typesetter:	Technical Typesetting Inc.

When citing a university paper, please use the proper form. Remember to cite the Sage University Paper series title and include paper number. One of the following formats can be adapted (depending on the style manual used):

(1) MARSH and CORMIER (2001) *Spline Regression Models.* Sage University Papers Series on Quantitative Applications in the Social Sciences, 07-137. Thousand Oaks, CA: Sage.

OR

(2) Marsh and Cormier (2001). *Spline Regression Models.* (Sage University Papers Series on Quantitative Applications in the Social Sciences, series no. 07-137). Thousand Oaks, CA: Sage.

CONTENTS

Series Editor's Introduction   v

1. General Introduction   1

Polynomial Regression Models   3
Spline Knot Locations Known in Advance   3
Splines With Unknown Knot Locations   5
Unknown Number of Spline Knots   6

2. Introduction to Spline Models   6

Interrupted Regression Analysis   7
Piecewise Linear Regression   9
Cubic Polynomial Regression   13
Important Features of Spline Models   14

3. Splines With Known Knot Locations   16

Linear Spline Regression Models   16
Quadratic and Higher Order Spline Regression Models   23
Hybrid Spline Regression Models   24
Model Comparison Issues   25
Model Selection Criteria   27
Polynomial Regression and Perfect Multicollinearity   31
F Statistics and t Statistics   31
Autocorrelation and the Durbin–Watson Statistic   32

4. Splines With Unknown Knot Locations   33

Transforming Discrete Response Into Continuous Measure   33
Interrupted Regression Analysis   35
Adjusting Intercepts Only   36
Adjusting Intercepts and Slopes   38
Splines With Known Knot Locations   39
Unknown Spline Knot Location Estimation   43

Quadratic Spline With Unknown Knot Locations 46
The Wald Test 48
Model Selection Conclusion 48

5. Splines With an Unknown Number of Knots 49

Stepwise Regression as a Powerful Nonparametric Method 49
Determining the Number, Location, and Degree of the
    Spline Knots 52
Smooth Splines for Long-Term Investing 53
Moderately Sensitive Splines for Medium-Term Investing 55
Highly Sensitive Splines for Short-Term Investing 56
Spline Regression Forecasting 58

6. Summary and Conclusions 61

Appendix: SAS® Program to Calculate Standard Error 63

Notes 65

References 67

About the Authors 69

SERIES EDITOR'S INTRODUCTION

Regression analysis has many variants. A useful but rather neglected one is spline regression. A family of techniques are relevant for spline models, including dummy variables, time counters, intervention analysis, interrupted time series, and piecewise linear models. [In this series, on dummy variables see Hardy, No. 93; on intervention analysis and interrupted time series, see McDowall, No. 21]. Suppose a continuous variable, Y, appears to change its trajectory over time in response to some event or policy. Take a concrete example, where Y (a state's annual welfare case load) experiences a steady rise over the years, then declines, apparently because of a newly implemented welfare reform. If the case load drops abruptly, then an interrupted time series design, which captures intercept shifts, might be appropriate. However, if the case load "damps off" rather than "drops off," a spline model is preferable, capturing the slope change smoothly in joining two regression lines without a break.

In this simple model, $Y = a + bT + cD(T - T_1) + e$, where Y is the annual welfare caseload, T is the time counter across the years in the series, $1, 2, \ldots N$; D is a dummy scored 0 in the years before the reform and 1 for the years thereafter; T_1 is the count corresponding to the year of the reform so that $D(T - T_1) = 1, 2, 3 \ldots$ is a count of the number of years since the reform. Say the "spline knot," the time when the reform occurred, was 1990. Then estimation of the model would yield two linear regressions before and after 1990 with no jump in the trend.

Spline regression is a general technique for fitting and smoothing the twists and turns of a time line. It is simplest when the spline knots are few and known in advance. Professor Marsh and Professor Cormier here give an illustration of changing voter party identification in response to political campaign changes at three distinct dates on the election calendar. They go on to develop a more complicated example of the interest rate on bonds as determined by the political party in the White House in an annual time series from 1890, where 11 party shifts (Republican to Democrat or vice versa) occurred. In the course of that example, they also demonstrate the poor performance of the chief rival modeling approach—polynomial regression, which here and elsewhere generally suffers from crippling multicollinearity problems.

Spline modeling becomes more difficult if the location of the knots is unknown, because then nonlinear least squares must be used. To illustrate this procedure, the authors examine the impact of three (unknown) ages on individual religious feeling. The illustration is also useful in showing that cross-sectional, as well as time series, data are subject to such analysis. Modeling complications further increase when the number of knots is unknown. To solve this problem, Marsh and Cormier experiment with a stepwise strategy that makes a statistical search through a host of possible knots in time series data on CREF stock growth. Most spline models are amenable to estimation with usual regression software packages. Hence, computation itself is no impediment. Especially when the research question is, "Did some X produce a change in slope?," the analyst should consider estimation of a spline regression, after consulting this readable little handbook.

—*Michael S. Lewis-Beck*
Series Editor

SPLINE REGRESSION MODELS

LAWRENCE C. MARSH
University of Notre Dame

DAVID R. CORMIER
Indiana University, Kokomo

1. GENERAL INTRODUCTION

Although spline regression models might sound like something complicated and formidable, they are really just dummy variable models with a few simple restrictions placed on them. In fact, spline models are dummy variable models subject to one or more continuity restriction.

For example, a politician's approval ratings might be highest when elected (or reelected) and tend to fall somewhat thereafter. This may be represented by a downward sloping regression line. However, at some point the politician may recognize the need to intensify efforts to regain public support before the next election. Using unrestricted dummy variables, the postelection model may have a different intercept and slope than the preelection model as shown in Figure 1.1.

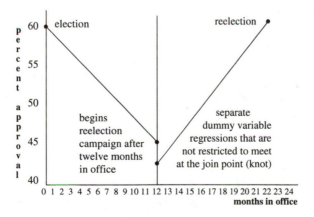

Figure 1.1. Unrestricted Dummy Variable Model of Approval Ratings

A spline regression model avoids the inappropriate "jump" (i.e., break) in joining the two regression lines. In a spline model, a turning point in the approval ratings is represented by a spline knot, which joins the downward regression line to the upward regression line as shown in Figure 1.2.

This type of spline model is often referred to as a piecewise linear regression model, and has been simply, yet carefully, explained by Pindyck and Rubinfeld (1998) as well as in earlier editions of their widely used textbook. Suits, Mason, and Chan (1978) provided more details in another clear and straightforward presentation of spline regression models. For an income tax application using this type of spline, see Strawczynski (1998), who used piecewise linear regression to account for the different tax brackets.

Thus, the regression line for the dependent variable of interest (e.g., approval rating) may suddenly change its slope without causing an abrupt "jump" in the line itself. This is accomplished by allowing a kink in the line (a change in the slope) without allowing a break in the line. This amounts to forcing the two separate regression lines to touch at their join point (spline knot) while their slopes are allowed to be different at that point.

Pindyck and Rubinfeld (1998) provided a brief discussion of the construction and use of a basic spline model with an example that

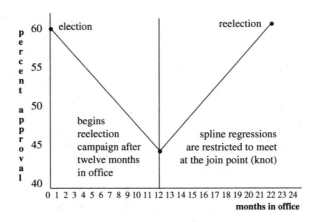

Figure 1.2. Spline Regression Model of Approval Ratings

demonstrates the use of these methods in a practical context. For a more detailed discussion of how to set up spline regression models, see the pioneering work of Smith (1979), who developed the simple adjustment approach to spline models.

Polynomial Regression Models

An obvious question is why not just use a polynomial regression model instead of splines? A polynomial regression model would have time, time-squared, time-cubed, and so forth as independent variables. The problem with polynomial regression is that it runs into perfect multicollinearity quite quickly as terms are added. In low dimensions, polynomial regressions are not flexible enough to capture sudden changes in slope, especially at irregular intervals. In high dimensions, polynomial regressions tend to fail due to perfect multicollinearity as will be demonstrated in Chapter 3. In contrast, spline regression models have substantially greater flexibility than polynomial regression models in low dimensions and are generally less likely to generate perfect multicollinearity in higher dimensions. Other methods such as kernel regression could be used, but Carroll (2000) reported that spline methods are generally more efficient than kernel methods. In addition, spline methods tend to be easier to use with standard regression packages (i.e., SPSS, SAS, etc.) than kernel methods.

Spline Knot Locations Known in Advance

The easiest situation is where the exact locations of the spline knots are known in advance. For example, the date that an energy tax credit or some other change in the tax law becomes effective is determined by Congress, so the knot location is known because the regression that explains energy related expenditures changes when the energy tax credit becomes law.

In another example, a psychologist might be interested in how a person's decision to lose weight at a given point in time translates over time into actual weight loss. The person's weight could serve as the dependent variable in a regression where time is the explanatory variable. If the psychologist knows when the person decided to go on a diet, then he or she knows the exact location of the knot or joint point.

Allsop and Weisberg (1988) provided an interesting example of the use of spline regression analysis in their research on tracking changes in party identification during the 1984 U.S. presidential election campaign. Their research indicated the presence of three spline knots located at June 19, September 12, and October 10. Using these three spline knots, they estimated four linear regressions that were connected so that no breaks existed in the overall curve. Their dependent variable, Y_t, was a questionnaire response that ranged from a minimum value of 1 if the respondent indicated that he or she was a strong Republican to a maximum of 5 if he or she was a strong Democrat. Allsop and Weisberg used time since the start of the election campaign, t, as their independent variable in the equation

$$Y_t = a_0 + b_0 t + b_1 D_{1t}(t-t_1) + b_2 D_{2t}(t-t_2) + b_3 D_{3t}(t-t_3) + e_t, \quad (1.1)$$

where t_1, t_2, and t_3 are the number of days since the beginning of the election campaign at June 19, September 12, and October 10, respectively. D_{1t}, D_{2t}, and D_{3t} are all equal to 0 when the number of days since the beginning of the campaign, t, is less than t_1, t_2, and t_3, respectively, and equal to 1 when t is greater than t_1, t_2, and t_3, respectively. Using this technology, Allsop and Weisberg (1988) were able to show that there were, indeed, four distinct phases in the 1984 election. Their spline model improved the R-squared of .242 from a simple regression over time to an R-squared of .323 for their spline regression for a $33\frac{1}{2}\%$ improvement in fit. We will assume that the researcher wants the smoothest possible spline for each case. For the linear case, this just means that the functions are forced to be equal at the join points, but their slopes are allowed to be different.

In the quadratic case both the functions and their slopes are equal at the join points, but the rate of change of their slopes is different. In the Allsop and Weisberg example, this would simply involve replacing the three linear independent variables $D_{1t}(t-t_1)$, $D_{2t}(t-t_2)$, and $D_{3t}(t-t_3)$ with the three corresponding quadratic independent variables $D_{1t}(t-t_1)^2$, $D_{2t}(t-t_2)^2$, and $D_{3t}(t-t_3)^2$.

In the cubic spline case, we restrict the functions as well as their slopes and the rate of change of their slopes, but allow for different *rates of change in the rate of change* of their slopes by simply replacing the three independent variables with the three cubic variables $D_{1t}(t-t_1)^3$, $D_{2t}(t-t_2)^3$, and $D_{3t}(t-t_3)^3$. Cubic splines are popular with people who want a very smooth, yet very flexible, fit to the data. Detailed discussions of cubic splines as a special case of restricted least squares can be found in Poirier (1973) and Buse and Lim (1977).

Although we did not attempt to replicate the Allsop and Weisberg results, we do provide a detailed analysis in Chapter 2 of a similar problem that involves election and reelection approval ratings.

Chapter 3 addresses the research question as to whether interest rates tend to go up (or down) more in a Republican administration than in a Democratic administration. In particular, Chapter 3 uses the 11 times that the White House changed hands since 1890 as spline knots that separate the 12 corresponding interest rate "regimes" or "spline segments." We then test to see if there is a statistically significant difference in interest rate behavior in Republican versus Democratic administrations.

Splines With Unknown Knot Locations

In all of the preceding examples, we assumed that the exact locations of the spline knots were known in advance. However, often we need to estimate spline models with unknown knot locations. This means that the join points are not known in advance and must be estimated from the data.

For example, by examining the approval ratings of successful politicians, a neophyte may be able to determine the optimal point (knot) to switch from the job of governing to the job of running for reelection. This determination involves estimating the unknown location of the spline knot. In the Ice Age, a fundamental change in regime occurred when temperatures stopped falling and began to rise. The exact turning point may not be obvious, so a spline model can be used to find it. Stock prices go up and down everyday, so when does a bull market become a bear market? When does a wheat crop go from having too little water to having too much water? The knot locations that define these unknown turning points must be estimated along with the regression coefficients of the model.

When the knot locations are unknown, the regression model becomes nonlinear in its parameters. Consequently, a nonlinear estimation method such as nonlinear least squares must be used. Chapter 4 provides an example of using nonlinear least squares in a search for the location of three spline knots. In particular, Chapter 4 addresses the research question of whether a person's commitment to religion varies with age and what three ages might be pivotal in understanding the changing relationship between age and religious commitment.

Unknown Number of Spline Knots

Chapter 5 presents an example, using time series data, of how to search for the number, location, and degree of the spline knots. A stepwise regression is used to determine the number, degree, and the location of the spline knots using Smith's adjustment approach. First introduced by Patricia Smith in 1979, the adjustment approach provides a framework that allows for the estimation of the number, location, and degree of the knots in a spline regression model. When the number, location, and degree of the knots are unknown, the model becomes nonparametric, and its structure must be estimated from sample data. First, using Smith's adjustment approach, we start with the case where the number, location, and degree of the knots are known. Then we address the unknown number, location, and degree case, and demonstrate a stepwise regression method for dealing with this problem.

Finally, Chapter 6 summarizes and reiterates the relationships between and among the various dummy variable based models we discussed. By comparing and contrasting their similarities and differences, we hope to clarify issues related to formulating, estimating, and interpreting such models. We hope that the blend of conceptual overview and technical detail with carefully selected examples in this document provides researchers with the ability to make effective use of these methods in practical applications. For example, for a useful application using splines in demography, see McNeil, Trussell, and Turner (1977).

2. INTRODUCTION TO SPLINE MODELS

Within the context of regression analysis, there is a close relationship between dummy variable models, intervention/interrupted models, and spline models (including piecewise linear models). Dummy variable regression models contain two or more distinct regression lines that correspond to two or more distinct classifications for the observed data points. The observations are divided into groups according to the value of a particular nominal, ordinal, or continuous variable (at cutoff points) or some linear combination of continuous variables. For example, the value of the nominal variable gender may place an observation in either a male grouping or a female grouping with two separate corresponding regression lines. Alternatively, for a given prespecified cutoff point, the value of the continuous variable income may place an observation in the low income class or the high income class for two separate regressions, or low, medium, and high income classes for three separate regressions. For an example that uses income tax categories, see Kanbur (1983).

Interrupted Regression Analysis

Interrupted regression uses dummy variables to produce an intervention component that can be either gradual or abrupt and either permanent or temporary. Lewis-Beck (1986) provided examples of both simple interrupted times series (SITS) to account for the impact of a single event and multiple interrupted time series (MITS) to account for the effects of more than one event. In his SITS example, Lewis-Beck uses January 8, 1959 to separate Cuban prerevolutionary from postrevolutionary energy consumption, and he finds an abrupt increase in intercept (greater immediate consumption), but a decrease in slope (a decrease in the rate of consumption). Lewis-Beck also discussed the impact on vehicle fatalities of hypothetical changes in the speed limit in Kentucky using SITS for a single such change and MITS for two such changes at different points in time. These changes can be expected to induce abrupt changes in both the intercept and the slope of the regression line. In an analysis of the impact of coal mining safety legislation on coal mine fatalities, Lewis-Beck found that the 1941 safety law produced a downward sloping regression line that substantially leveled off after the 1952 law was passed, but again sloped downward after the 1969 legislation. McDowall, McCleary, Meidinger, and Hay (1980) discussed the application of interrupted regression to ARIMA (autoregressive integrated moving average) time series analysis. Their model-building approach focuses on identification, estimation, and diagnosis of intervention components in interrupted time series models.

When a continuous variable is broken up into different groupings or segments, a question may arise as to whether the model should remain a strict intervention/interrupted regression model with abrupt breaks in the function with or without changes in the slopes of the

8

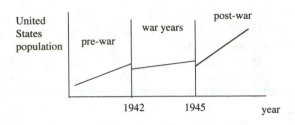

Figure 2.1. Unrestricted Interrupted Model of War–Peace Population

segments, or whether it should be transformed into a spline regression model. The essential difference between intervention/interrupted regressions and spline regressions is that intervention/interrupted regression methods emphasize abrupt changes, whereas splines focus on smoother transitions. Splines are defined as functions that are continuous (no visible breaks allowed) but change in more subtle ways at specific points known as spline knots.

For example, Figure 2.1 depicts a separate regression line with different slopes for the United States population for the three time periods of pre-World War II, during World War II, and after World War II. Using an unrestricted version of intervention/interrupted regression, the prewar model may have a different intercept and slope than either the war model or the postwar model as shown in Figure 2.1. This contrasts with the spline model (or restricted version of the intervention/interrupted model) as shown in Figure 2.2, where the function itself is forced to be continuous at the knot or join point locations, whereas its slope may be discontinuous at these points.

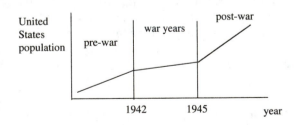

Figure 2.2. Spline (Restricted Interrupted) Model of War–Peace Population

These join points separate the different regression piecewise linear segments depicted in Figure 2.2.

Piecewise Linear Regression

A piecewise linear spline model can be defined as a regression model that consists of a continuous explanatory variable defined over specified segments of the domain of that variable and a dependent variable that is a continuous function of that explanatory variable over all segments, but with different slopes in each of the separate segments. In Figure 2.2, the function is continuous, but its slope in the different segments (i.e., the regression line slopes) is discontinuous at the two prespecified knot locations x_1 (=1942) and x_2 (=1945). This is a special type of spline model known as a piecewise linear regression model.

Spline regression models are used when a regression line is broken into a number of line segments separated by special join points known as spline *knots*. The regression line changes direction at these join points, but does not "jump" at these points. If the regression line is discontinuous (jumps) at the join points, then a simple dummy variable model that allows each line segment to have its own intercept and slope will work fine. However, often having discontinuities at the join points does not make sense. For example, if a person is gaining weight over time, but suddenly decides to lose weight, then— barring liposuction—his or her weight should drop gradually. In other words, he or she must start with the weight he or she currently has. There is no instantaneous drop in weight at the moment the decision is made to lose weight. Hence, splines are used to impose continuity restrictions at the join points so that the line can change direction without inappropriate jumps in the line at those join points. For an application concerning housing prices and flood risk, see Speyrer and Ragas (1991).

Pindyck and Rubinfeld (1998) introduced splines in their textbook under the heading "Piecewise Linear Regression," which is a good description of the simplest spline models, which, in effect, piece together two or more linear regressions. The example they presented views private consumption expenditures as being disrupted at the start of World War II and, then again, at the end of the war. The spline knot adjustments that they introduced allow the linear consumption relationship to remain continuous (i.e., no breaks) with a slope adjustment at the start of the war and another one at the end. In effect, a lot of private consumption was held in abeyance during the war. Consequently, the consumption relationship was nearly horizontal during the war, but regained its upward direction, a fortiori, after the war. Because this pattern is very similar to the U.S. birth rate and population changes during the war, Figures 2.1 and 2.2 again provide a general picture.

The following hypothetical example demonstrates the use of a piecewise linear spline model. A member of the U.S. House of Representatives is concerned about his or her approval ratings. This politician wants to see how the percentage of the electorate that approves of his or her performance in office is changing over time. The politician's percentage approval rating is regressed on time in office in months. The regression produces an insignificant slope coefficient and a very low R-squared as seen in Figure 2.3.

Once elected, a politician has to focus on the job of evaluating and proposing legislation. After about half of the 2-year term in office, the politician realizes that he or she must shift time and effort toward running for reelection. At that point he or she starts to spend more time back in his or her district and allocates more time and effort, in this regard, as the election date gets closer and closer. For an efficient politician, this cycle produces a high in his or her approval ratings at the time of election. Figure 2.4 shows simulated data that display

Source	DF	Sum of Squares	Mean Square	F Value	Prob>F
Model	1	124.39847	124.39847	3.385	0.0709
Error	58	2131.59027	36.75156		
C Total	59	2255.98875			

Root MSE	6.06231	R-square	0.0551	
Dep Mean	48.38464	Adj R-sq	0.0389	
C.V.	12.52940			

Parameter Estimates

Variable	DF	Parameter Estimate	Standard Error	T for H0: Parameter=0	Prob > |T|
INTERCEP	1	45.550099	1.72806826	26.359	0.0001
MONTHS	1	0.107007	0.05816253	1.840	0.0709

Figure 2.3. Approval Rating Simple Regression Output

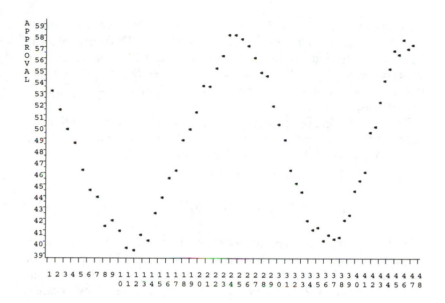

Figure 2.4. Percent Approval Versus Months in Office

this pattern, ranging from a high of nearly 60% approval to a low of around 40%. These types of data are likely to occur when well-defined behavior generates turning points in a manner that is crisp (sudden change in slope), but not abrupt (no break or jump in the line).

As Pindyck and Rubinfeld (1998) demonstrate, the first step in setting up a spline model is to create special dummy variables that take on the value 0 before the spline adjustment date (i.e., spline knot) and a value of 1 thereafter. By looking at Figure 2.4 we can see that we need spline knots at 12, 24, and 36 months in office. Consequently, we need to create the three dummy variables D_{1t}, D_{2t}, and D_{3t} based on the value of months in office, X_t. More specifically, for the first dummy variable, when $X_t \leq 12$, then $D_{1t} = 0$, and when $X_t > 12$, then $D_{1t} = 1$. For the second dummy variable, when $X_t \leq 24$, then $D_{2t} = 0$, and when $X_t > 24$, then $D_{2t} = 1$. Finally, for the third dummy variable, when $X_t \leq 36$, then $D_{3t} = 0$, and when $X_t > 36$, then $D_{3t} = 1$.

Using the first dummy variable, D_{1t}, we can create the corresponding spline adjustment variable Z_{1t} as $Z_{1t} = D_{1t}(X_t - 12)$. Notice that whenever X_t is less than 12, $D_{1t} = 0$, so Z_{1t} can never be negative.

Furthermore, Z_{1t} is equal to 0 at $X_t = 12$, but takes on values $1, 2, 3, \ldots$ as X_t takes on values $13, 14, 15, \ldots$. Thus, the effect of Z_{1t} is introduced gradually as X_t moves beyond 12. In a similar way, we can create $Z_{2t} = D_{2t}(X_t - 24)$ and $Z_{3t} = D_{3t}(X_t - 36)$, which operate in a similar manner relative to their spline knot values of 24 and 36, respectively.

The spline regression model now consists of a linear relationship between the politician's approval rating, Y_t, and his or her months in office, X_t, along with the three spline adjustment variables, Z_{1t}, Z_{2t}, and Z_{3t}, as expressed in the equation

$$Y_t = a_0 + b_0 X_t + b_1 Z_{1t} + b_2 Z_{2t} + b_3 Z_{3t} + e_t, \qquad (2.1)$$

where a_0 is the intercept or constant term, $b_0, b_1, b_2,$ and b_3 are regression slope coefficients, and e_t is the regression error term assumed to satisfy all of the usual assumptions. Under these circumstances, Equation 2.1 can be appropriately estimated by ordinary linear least squares.

By running this piecewise linear regression, the politician gets results that show that approval rating fluctuations can be explained quite well by the dates of reelection and 1 year after reelection.

Figure 2.5 reveals that the overall statistical significance of the spline regression is quite strong, with an F statistic of 321.32 and a p value smaller than .0001. The R-squared of .959 is good with large t statistics and corresponding p values that are all smaller than .0001. The slope coefficients alternate in sign and demonstrate dramatic changes in direction at 12, 24, and 36 months. By substituting into Equation 2.1 for Z_{1t}, Z_{2t}, and Z_{3t} and using the three spline knots, the time data may be divided into the following four periods:

Months 0 through 12:

$$Y_t = a_0 + b_0 X_t + e_t \qquad (2.2a)$$
$$= 54.764042 - 1.434123 X_t + e_t. \qquad (2.2b)$$

Months 13 through 24:

$$Y_t = (a_0 - 12b_1) + (b_0 + b_1)X_t + e_t \qquad (2.3a)$$
$$= 15.382238 + 1.847694 X_t + e_t. \qquad (2.3b)$$

Source	DF	Sum of Squares	Mean Square	F Value	Prob>F
Model	4	2163.41179	540.85295	321.321	0.0001
Error	55	92.57696	1.68322		
C Total	59	2255.98875			

Root MSE	1.29739	R-square	0.9590	
Dep Mean	48.38464	Adj R-sq	0.9560	
C.V.	2.68141			

Parameter Estimates

Variable	DF	Parameter Estimate	Standard Error	T for H0: Parameter=0	Prob > |T|
INTERCEP	1	54.764042	0.80711054	67.852	0.0001
MONTHS	1	-1.434123	0.09194544	-15.598	0.0001
Z1	1	3.281817	0.13924890	23.568	0.0001
Z2	1	-3.578081	0.10872502	-32.909	0.0001
Z3	1	3.466670	0.11508387	30.123	0.0001

Figure 2.5. Spline Regression Output

Months 25 through 36:

$$Y_t = (a_0 - 12b_1 - 24b_2) + (b_0 + b_1 + b_2)X_t + e_t \tag{2.4a}$$

$$= 101.256182 - 1.730387X_t + e_t. \tag{2.4b}$$

Months 37 through 48:

$$Y_t = (a_0 - 12b_1 - 24b_2 - 36b_3) + (b_0 + b_1 + b_2 + b_3)X_t + e_t \tag{2.5a}$$

$$= -23.543938 + 1.736283X_t + e_t. \tag{2.5b}$$

Moreover, the ability of the spline regression to efficiently use the turning point information is clearly demonstrated in Figure 2.6.

Cubic Polynomial Regression

In contrast, the output for a cubic polynomial model is provided in Figure 2.7, which corresponds to the equation

$$Y_t = \delta_1 + \delta_2 X_t + \delta_3 X_t^2 + \delta_4 X_t^3 + e_t. \tag{2.6}$$

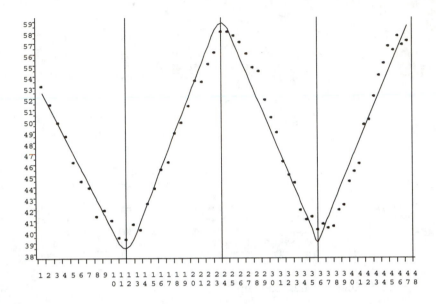

Figure 2.6. Spline Regression Approval Rating Versus Months in Office

With an insignificant F statistic of 1.88, an R-squared of only .0915, and t statistics that all suggest that the population coefficient values are all zero, the cubic polynomial is clearly not an adequate alternative.

To achieve an R-squared as good as the spline model requires a polynomial with at least seven terms (i.e., seven independent variables). In other words, a higher order polynomial ultimately could fit these data adequately, but only at the cost of using up more degrees of freedom. Furthermore, polynomial regressions would have an even harder time fitting a model where the turning points are not evenly spaced, whereas a spline regression model easily could accommodate such a circumstance.

Important Features of Spline Models

In applying spline methods, three features of splines play an important role: (1) the number of distinct spline segments into which the independent variable falls, (2) the degree of the polynomial used to represent each segment, and (3) the location of the segment join

Source	DF	Sum of Squares	Mean Square	F Value	Prob>F
Model	3	206.46895	68.82298	1.880	0.1434
Error	56	2049.51980	36.59857		
C Total	59	2255.98875			

Root MSE	6.04968	R-square	0.0915	
Dep Mean	48.38464	Adj R-sq	0.0429	
C.V.	12.50330			

Parameter Estimates

Variable	DF	Parameter Estimate	Standard Error	T for H0: Parameter=0	Prob > |T|
INTERCEP	1	42.458010	4.07035879	10.431	0.0001
MONTHS	1	0.877186	0.67957374	1.291	0.2021
MONTHS2	1	-0.041022	0.03113430	-1.318	0.1930
MONTHS3	1	0.000581	0.00041167	1.412	0.1634

Figure 2.7. Cubic Polynomial Regression Output

points (i.e., the spline knots). The selection of the appropriate spline model to be used is influenced by whether or not these aspects are known a priori or are unknown. If one or more of these features is unknown, then it must be estimated as a parameter of the regression model. As we show, these are critical factors that influence the choice of the method of solution.

The simplest case is where the number of segments, the degree, and the location of the knots are assumed to be known. This case is presented in Chapter 3. Then, in Chapter 4, the location of the knots is considered to be unknown. In other words, the number and degree of the splines are known, but where they join is assumed to be unknown. Two situations can arise in the case of unknown knot locations. The easier of the two is where the number of segments is known, but exactly where they join is not. The more complicated case is when the number of segments is unknown, which generally implies that the knot locations must necessarily be unknown as well. The former case is more straightforward and is the case explained in Chapter 4. The latter is more difficult to estimate and is discussed in Chapter 5.

3. SPLINES WITH KNOWN KNOT LOCATIONS

In the first part of this chapter we consider linear spline models. Later on, we examine quadratic, cubic, and higher order spline models. Splines are easiest to use when the points where the regression line changes are known in advance. These join points, or spline knots, come directly from the specifics of the particular application of interest. Consequently, to illustrate the specification, estimation, and interpretation of spline regressions with known spline knot locations, we use the example of how interest rates are affected by which political party controls the White House. The research question here is, "Do interest rates behave differently under Republican versus Democratic administrations?" In particular, are the regression line slopes significantly different from one another in a regression of interest rates versus time expressed in years? The dependent variable is the annualized interest rate on 6-month commercial bonds. These data were obtained from the Federal Reserve web site. The key independent variable is time in years, starting with 1890. The spline knots are the years when the White House changed from Republican to Democrat or vice versa. At the time of this writing, there were 11 such changes since 1890, producing spline knots at 1892, 1896, 1912, 1920, 1932, 1952, 1960, 1968, 1976, 1980, and 1992.

Linear Spline Regression Models

To set up the appropriate spline model, we must first create a special set of dummy variables. For convenience, we name these dummy variables D1892, R1896, D1912, R1920, D1932, R1952, D1960, R1968, D1976, R1980, and D1992, where the leading "D" means that the Democrats took over the White House that year, whereas the leading "R" means that the Republicans took over. These dummy variables have a value of 0 before reaching the designated year and a value of 1, thereafter. For example, $D1892_t = 0$ for the years before 1892, and $D1892_t = 1$ for the years 1892 to 2000. Each of the other dummy variables is defined in an analogous manner. The original model, before incorporating the spline adjustments, is given by

$$Y_t = a_0 + b_0 X_t + e_t, \tag{3.1}$$

where Y_t is the annualized interest rate on 6-month commercial bonds in percentage terms (i.e., multiplied by 100) and X_t is time expressed as years starting with $X_t = 1890$.

Before considering a spline model, it is natural to try a plain old polynomial regression (nonspline) model. This simply involves extending Equation 3.1 to include additional terms for X^2, X^3, X^4, ... Using a polynomial to the 12th power, we found that we had a great deal of perfect multicollinearity among the various polynomial terms. In fact, of the 12 polynomial terms, only three of them could be used because the other nine were perfectly correlated with those three. The graph of the resulting polynomial function is displayed in Figure 3.1.

The poor performance of the polynomial regression model opens the way for consideration of a spline model as an alternative. Including $D1892_t$ through $D1992_t$ as additional independent variables on the right side of Equation 3.1 would adjust the constant term a_0, but this would not be appropriate because it is the slope coefficient b_0 that tells us how interest rates change over time. We make the standard assumptions about the error term, e_t, including the optional

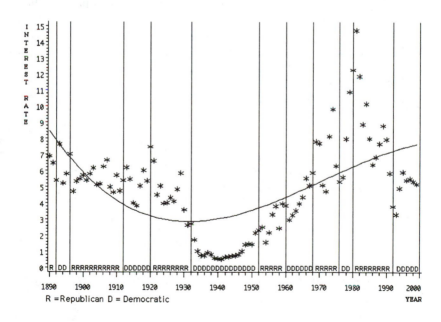

Figure 3.1. Polynomial (Nonspline) Model of Interest Rates

18

assumption that the errors are normally distributed which we need for hypothesis testing.[1] Consequently, we must create appropriate independent variables to adjust b_0 at each of the designated spline knots shown in Figure 3.2 and specified in the equation

$$
\begin{aligned}
Y_t = {} & a_0 + b_0 X_t + b_1 \text{D}1892_t(X_t - 1892) + b_2 \text{R}1896_t(X_t - 1896) \\
& + b_3 \text{D}1912_t(X_t - 1912) + b_4 \text{R}1920_t(X_t - 1920) \\
& + b_5 \text{D}1932_t(X_t - 1932) + b_6 \text{R}1952_t(X_t - 1952) \\
& + b_7 \text{D}1960_t(X_t - 1960) + b_8 \text{R}1968_t(X_t - 1968) \\
& + b_9 \text{D}1976_t(X_t - 1976) + b_{10} \text{R}1980_t(X_t - 1980) \\
& + b_{11} \text{D}1992_t(X_t - 1992) + e_t.
\end{aligned} \tag{3.2}
$$

Equation 3.2 allows for an adjustment to the slope of the regression line whenever a new political party takes over the White House. However, it does not permit a break in the regression line. At the moment that $\text{D}1892_t$ turns from 0 to 1, the year is $X_t = 1892$ so that $(X_t - 1892) = 0$. Consequently, there is no jump in the

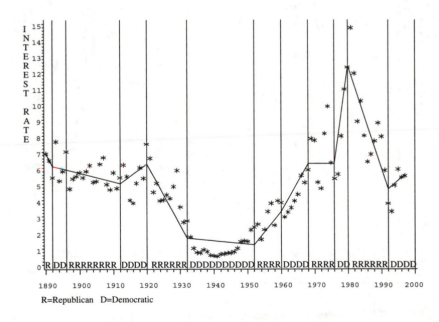

Figure 3.2. Interest Rate on 6-Month Commercial Bonds by Year

interest rate, Y_t, at that point. In other words, before the year 1892, the term $D1892_t(X_t - 1892)$ is 0 because $D1892_t = 0$. At the year 1892, the term $D1892_t(X_t - 1892)$ is 0 because $(X_t - 1892) = 0$. After the year 1892, the term $D1892_t(X_t - 1892)$ gradually increases to 1, 2, 3,... as X_t takes on the values 1893, 1894, 1895,....

It is important to recognize that Equation 3.2 actually represents 12 separate equations that correspond to the various Republican and Democratic administrations with intercepts c_0, c_1, c_2,..., c_{11} and slopes d_0, d_1, d_2,..., d_{11} as follows:

Republicans rule (1889–1892; our data actually start in 1890):

$$Y_t = a_0 + b_0 X_t + e_t = c_0 + d_0 X_t + e_t$$

Democrats rule (1893–1896):

$$Y_t = (a_0 - 1892b_1) + (b_0 + b_1)X_t + e_t = c_1 + d_1 X_t + e_t$$

Republicans rule (1897–1912):

$$Y_t = (a_0 - 1892b_1 - 1896b_2) + (b_0 + b_1 + b_2)X_t + e_t$$
$$= c_2 + d_2 X_t + e_t$$

Democrats rule (1913–1920):

$$Y_t = (a_0 - 1892b_1 - 1896b_2 - 1912b_3) + (b_0 + b_1 + b_2 + b_3)X_t + e_t$$

$$\vdots$$

Notice that the constant term has to be adjusted each time to accommodate the change in the slope. This keeps the regression line continuous (i.e., without a break in it) even as the regression line pivots to change direction at each spline knot as shown in Figure 3.2.

The regression results from estimating the spline regression represented by Equation 3.2 are presented in Figure 3.3. The left column lists the variable name, followed by the degrees of freedom (DF), used to estimate its coefficient. The third column designates "R" for Republican administration and "D" for Democratic administration. The R-squared of .8503 means that about 85% of the variation in the interest rate is explained by time measured in years with 11 spline knot adjustments. This is considerably better than a regression of interest rate on time in years alone which yields an R-squared of only .0369 or about 4%.

Dependent Variable: INTEREST

Analysis of Variance

Source	DF	Sum of Squares	Mean Square	F Value	Prob>F
Model	12	684.73344	57.06112	45.927	0.0001
Error	97	120.51584	1.24243		
C Total	109	805.24928			

Root MSE	1.11464	R-square	0.8503
Dep Mean	4.87045	Adj R-sq	0.8318
C.V.	22.88583		

Parameter Estimates

Variable	DF		Parameter Estimate	Standard Error	T for H0: Parameter=0	Prob>|T|
intercept	1		$737.556527 = a_0$	1298.2864057	0.568	0.5713
YEAR	1	R	$-0.386593 = b_0$	0.68648369	-0.563	0.5746
(X-1892)	1	D	$0.334461 = b_1$	0.85888919	0.389	0.6978
(X-1896)	1	R	$-0.002508 = b_2$	0.27397119	-0.009	0.9927
(X-1912)	1	D	$0.206833 = b_3$	0.12026596	1.720	0.0887
(X-1920)	1	R	$-0.534362 = b_4$	0.12848725	-4.159	0.0001
(X-1932)	1	D	$0.361257 = b_5$	0.07809608	4.626	0.0001
(X-1952)	1	R	$0.277766 = b_6$	0.10976580	2.531	0.0130
(X-1960)	1	D	$0.112986 = b_7$	0.17308623	0.653	0.5154
(X-1968)	1	R	$-0.368302 = b_8$	0.19172082	-1.921	0.0577
(X-1976)	1	D	$1.520613 = b_9$	0.29428174	5.167	0.0001
(X-1980)	1	R	$-2.155277 = b_{10}$	0.25710259	-8.383	0.0001
(X-1992)	1	D	$0.739743 = b_{11}$	0.18523753	3.993	0.0001

Durbin-Watson D	1.216
Number of Observations	110
1st Order Autocorrelation	0.391

Figure 3.3. Regression Results From Estimation Equation (3.2)

The constant term $a_0 = 737.56$ tells us the interest rate implied for the year zero. Whereas the year zero is outside the relevant range of 1890 to 2000, the constant term is not meaningful by itself; it only helps define the regression line for the initial segment from 1890 to 1892. Whereas the slope coefficient for the first segment is $b_0 = -0.3866$, the predicted interest rate for the year 1890 (i.e., $X_t = 1890$) is calculated to be $a_0 + b_0 X_t = 737.56 - 0.3866 \times 1890 = 6.89$, which is close to the actual 1890 interest rate of 6.91. The other regression parameters, b_1 through b_{11}, indicate how much each new administration contributed to changing the slope of the regression line. Using these regression parameters, we can calculate the slope coefficient for X_t corresponding to each Republican (R) or Democratic (D) administration as follows:

R, 1890–1892:
$$d_0 = b_0 = -0.386593;$$

D, 1893–1896:
$$d_1 = b_0 + b_1 = -0.052132;$$

R, 1897–1912:
$$d_2 = b_0 + b_1 + b_2 = 0.331953;$$

D, 1913–1920:
$$d_3 = b_0 + b_1 + b_2 + b_3 = 0.204325;$$

R, 1921–1932:
$$d_4 = b_0 + b_1 + b_2 + b_3 + b_4 = -0.327529;$$

D, 1933–1952:
$$d_5 = b_0 + b_1 + b_2 + b_3 + b_4 + b_5 = -0.173105;$$

R, 1953–1960:
$$d_6 = b_0 + b_1 + b_2 + b_3 + b_4 + b_5 + b_6 = 0.639023;$$

D, 1961–1968:
$$d_7 = b_0 + b_1 + b_2 + b_3 + b_4 + b_5 + b_6 + b_7 = 0.390752;$$

R, 1969–1976:
$$d_8 = b_0 + b_1 + b_2 + b_3 + b_4 + b_5 + b_6 + b_7 + b_8 = -0.255316;$$

D, 1977–1980:
$$d_9 = b_0 + b_1 + b_2 + b_3 + b_4 + b_5 + b_6 + b_7 + b_8 + b_9 = 1.152311;$$

R, 1981–1992:
$$d_{10} = b_0 + b_1 + b_2 + b_3 + b_4 + b_5 + b_6 + b_7 + b_8 + b_9 + b_{10}$$
$$= -0.634664;$$

D, 1993–2000:
$$d_{11} = b_0 + b_1 + b_2 + b_3 + b_4 + b_5 + b_6 + b_7 + b_8 + b_9 + b_{10} + b_{11}$$
$$= -1.415534.$$

We would like to test the null hypothesis that the average rate of change in interest rates (i.e., the average regression slope) during Republican administrations is the same as during Democratic administrations. The 11 spline knots define 12 segments that correspond to the 6 Republican administrations and 6 Democratic administrations. The null hypothesis that the average slope over the six Republican time segments is equal to the average slope over the six Democratic segments requires a test statistic. The test statistic is found by subtracting the average slope estimate during the Republican years from the average slope estimate during the Democratic years and then dividing by the appropriate standard error (see the SAS® program[2] in the Appendix).

The problem is complicated slightly by the fact that a straight average is not appropriate because the administrations were not in power exactly the same number of years. Consequently, we must set a weighted average of the Republican slopes equal to a weighted average of the Democratic slopes.[3] For the Republicans, multiplying the number of years times the calculated slope coefficients yields

$$[3d_0 + 16d_2 + 12d_4 + 8d_6 + 8d_8 + 12d_{10}]/59$$
$$= [3(-0.386593) + 16(0.331953) + 12(-0.327529) + 8(0.639023)$$
$$+ 8(-0.255316) + 12(-0.634664)]/59$$
$$= [-4.325191]/59 = -0.073308.$$

In other words, the (weighted) average slope for Republicans was -0.073308. Similarly for the Democrats, we have

$$[4d_1 + 8d_3 + 20d_5 + 8d_7 + 4d_9 + 7d_{11}]/51$$
$$= [4(-0.052132) + 8(0.204325) + 20(-0.173105) + 8(0.390752)$$
$$+ 4(1.152311) + 7(-1.415534)]/51$$
$$= [-4.209506]/51 = -0.082539.$$

In other words, the (weighted) average Democratic slope was -0.082539.

These data suggest that the fall in interest rates from 6.91% in 1890 to 5.18% in 1999 occurred during both Republican and Democratic administrations, but possibly more during Democratic ones. This last contention subsequently will be examined more closely to see if this difference is statistically significant.

These data provide a good example of the danger of using unweighted averages, because they tell an entirely different story than the weighted averages. The unweighted averages of -0.105521 for Republicans and 0.017770 for Democrats appear to suggest that interest rates fall during Republican administrations and rise during Democratic administrations. However, the weighted averages contradict this interpretation completely by suggesting that although interest rates tend to fall in Republican administrations, they actually fall even more during Democratic administrations.

Because the average interest rate in Republican years was 5.73% versus 3.87% in Democratic years, the weighted averages make more sense. The difference between the average weighted slope of the Democrats and that of the Republicans has a Student's t distribution with a standard error that was calculated using the SAS® program in the Appendix and has a resulting Student's t statistic value of -3.214. With 97 degrees of freedom the appropriate critical value at the 1% significance level is no farther from zero than -2.66, so the null hypothesis is rejected. The conclusion is that the average weighted slope of the Democrats' regression line is more steeply downward sloping than that of the Republicans in predicting interest rates over time. We have answered the research question in the context of a particular spline model, but in the next section we will examine the question of which spline model is best, given a number of attractive alternatives.

Quadratic and Higher Order Spline Regression Models

As noted in the previous section, the spline Equation 3.2 is a considerable improvement over the nonspline Equation 3.1. However, even with the improvement in the model's fit to the data, Figure 3.2 shows a piecewise linear spline model that does not pick up on the obviously nonlinear nature of the historical interest rate data. An alternative is to fit a quadratic or higher order spline model. In this section, we will consider alternative spline model specifications for this problem. At the end of the section, we will discuss the various criteria that might be used to choose between the alternative specifications. As we will see, there are no hard and fast rules, but rather some practical considerations and conceptual concerns that help guide our decision.

The quadratic spline equation model that is our first alternative to Equation 3.2 is

$$
\begin{aligned}
Y_t = a_0 + b_0 X_t &+ b_1 D1892_t (X_t - 1892)^2 + b_2 R1896_t (X_t - 1896)^2 \\
&+ b_3 D1912_t (X_t - 1912)^2 + b_4 R1920_t (X_t - 1920)^2 \\
&+ b_5 D1932_t (X_t - 1932)^2 + b_6 R1952_t (X_t - 1952)^2 \\
&+ b_7 D1960_t (X_t - 1960)^2 + b_8 R1968_t (X_t - 1968)^2 \\
&+ b_9 D1976_t (X_t - 1976)^2 + b_{10} R1980_t (X_t - 1980)^2 \\
&+ b_{11} D1992_t (X_t - 1992)^2 + e_t.
\end{aligned} \tag{3.3}
$$

Both the linear and the quadratic models avoid sudden breaks in the regression line, but the quadratic model also avoids any sudden changes in its slope. This means that the quadratic spline model allows only for breaks in the rate at which the slope itself changes and not in the slope itself. In other words, the model is continuous in the function and the rate of change of the function, but not in the rate of change of the rate of change of the function. This means that the quadratic spline model offers an intrinsically smoother regression line than the linear spline model. Figure 3.4 presents the results of the fit of Equation 3.3 to the interest rate data.

Alternatively, if we cube the terms in Equation 3.3 instead of squaring them, we can obtain the graph displayed in Figure 3.5. Raising the terms to the fourth power generates the quartic model shown in Figure 3.6. Extensions to higher order powers are certainly possible, but do not necessarily lead to better results.

Hybrid Spline Regression Models

Combining levels of smoothing can produce a hybrid spline model such as the quadratic–cubic spline model, which includes both the squared adjustment terms and the cubic adjustment terms in the same model. The graph for this quadratic–cubic spline model is shown in Figure 3.7.

We could join the quadratic spline model and the quartic spline model to produce the hybrid quadratic–quartic spline model displayed in Figure 3.8 or join the quadratic and quintic model to produce the hybrid quadratic–quintic model in Figure 3.9. Finally, we could combine linear, quadratic, and quintic terms to create the triple hybrid linear–quadratic–quintic model that generated Figure 3.10.

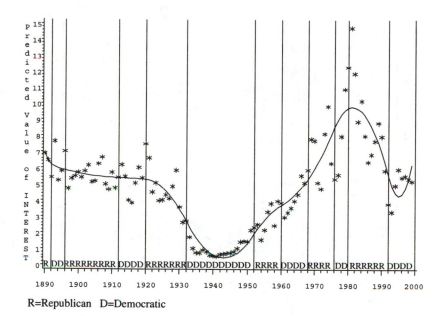

1890   1900   1910   1920   1930   1940   1950   1960   1970   1980   1990   2000

R=Republican   D=Democratic

Figure 3.4. Quadratic Spline Interest Rate Model

Model Comparison Issues

How then can we decide which model is best? The essential problem centers on the basic issue underlying the scientific method itself. The population is presumed to contain some systematic relationships that we would like to discover. Those population relationships hopefully are represented in any given sample. However, there are also some relationships in each sample that are unique to that sample and do not represent the population at all. The question is how to distinguish between the relationships in a particular sample that reflect population relationships and those that are unique to that particular sample. The scientific method was designed to deal with precisely this problem. Before performing an experiment (i.e., before looking at the sample data), chemistry students are obliged to write down on the left hand side of their chemistry notebook exactly how the experiment is to be performed as well as how each of the different possible outcomes would be interpreted. An extension of this method means we

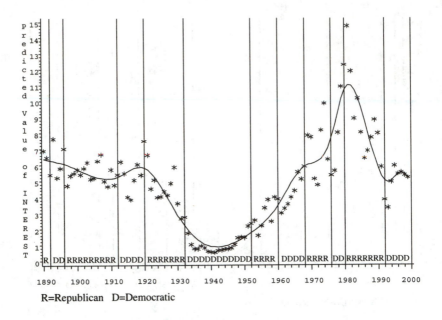

Figure 3.5. Cubic Spline Interest Rate Model

must specify our models, the error term assumptions we are making, and the levels of significance we will be using for any tests.

Only after the methodology is clearly and completely stated can we proceed with the experiment. On the right side of our notebook, we write down the details of the observed outcome from the experiment. The scientific method also has technical implications. For example, completely specifying our model before we actually estimate it is essential for Student's t and F distributions to hold up properly and to provide us with a confirmatory analysis. Otherwise, by trying on different model specifications, we are engaging in exploratory analysis that undermines and destroys the implicit distributional assumptions needed for proper Student's t and F tests and confidence intervals. The exploratory approach is sometimes referred to as pretesting. In practical terms, this means that we can rely on the t and F tests in the first round of estimation, but not in subsequent estimation that is performed conditional on the first round outcomes.

The foregoing discussion means that the problem boils down to the question of how to avoid overfitting to the sample. In other words,

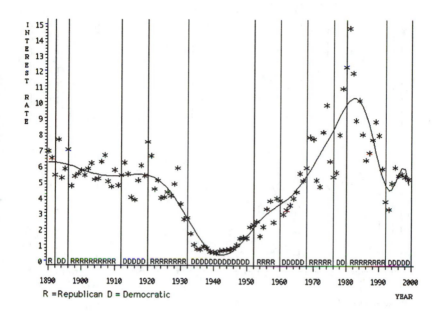

Figure 3.6. Quartic Spline Interest Rate Model

at what point should we stop making "improvements" to the model that lead to a better sample fit, but quite likely lead to a misleading or worse representation of the population data generating process. After all, overfitting can have disastrous implications both for interpolation within the range of the sample as well as for forecasting outside that range.

Model Selection Criteria

We now consider the basic model selection criteria. Although there are considerably more complicated model selection criteria available, we stick with the fundamental, tried-and-true methods of elementary regression analysis. In particular, we consider the coefficient of determination or R-squared, the adjusted R-squared, the F statistic, the set of t statistics, multicollinearity, autocorrelation, and a general sense of the extent to which the model and its fit to the data satisfy our theoretical and commonsense expectations.

28

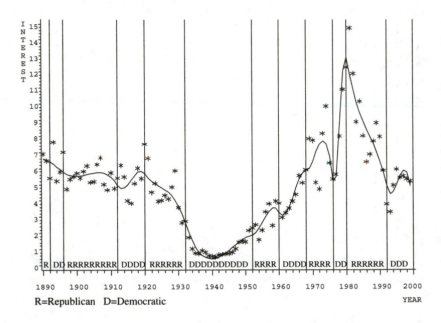

Figure 3.7. Quadratic–Cubic Spline Interest Rate Model

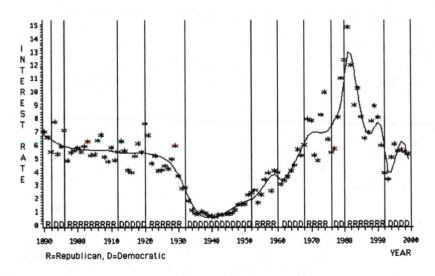

Figure 3.8. Quadratic–Quartic Spline Interest Rate Model

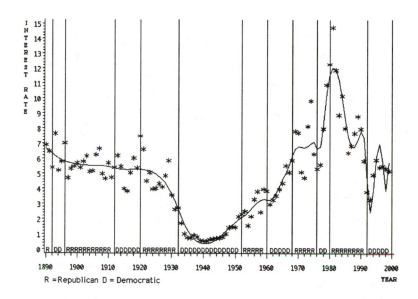

Figure 3.9. Quadratic–Quintic Spline Interest Rate Model

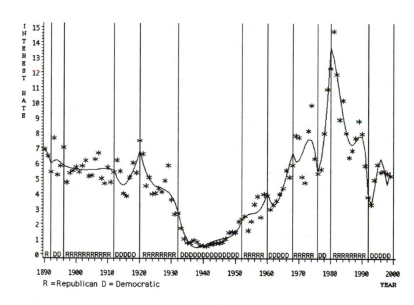

Figure 3.10. Linear–Quadratic–Quintic Spline Interest Rate Model

TABLE 3.1
Model Selection Comparison Criteria

Model	R^2	R^2-bar	F	Mult	Auto	Variables	Drop
Simple regression	.0369	.0279	4.133	1	0.217	1	0
Polynomial regression	.3661	.3481	20.404	9.3E−12	0.329	3	9
Linear spline	.8503	.8318	45.927	5.0E−24	1.216	12	0
Quadratic spline	.8156	.7928	35.748	1.9E−34	1.096	12	0
Cubic spline	.8386	.8187	42.006	1.6E−41	1.198	12	0
Quartic spline	.8271	.8057	38.657	1.3E−46	1.151	12	0
Quintic spline	.8308	.8099	39.698	2.1E−50	1.165	12	0
Quadratic–cubic	.8960	.8697	34.071	2.7E−92	1.683	22	2
Quadratic–quartic	.8851	.8561	30.467	3.3E−96	1.554	22	2
Quadratic–quintic	.8951	.8686	33.742	2.2E−97	1.711	22	2
Linear-quadratic–quintic	.9241	.8926	29.307	2.4E−132	2.139	32	4

The first column of Table 3.1 presents the different models we wish to compare. The second column presents the coefficient of determination or R-squared. The third column gives the adjusted R-squared known as R-bar-squared. The fourth column contains the F statistic, which provides an overall test of the model. The fifth column represents the degree of multicollinearity as measured by the determinant of the independent variables' correlation matrix. The sixth column provides the Durbin–Watson test statistic for autocorrelation. The seventh column reports the number of independent variables used in the regression, and the last column indicates the number of additional regressors that were dropped from the model because they were perfectly correlated with a linear combination of the independent variables remaining in the regression. In other words, the last column indicates the number of additional variables we tried to include but had to drop.

The first row corresponds to a simple regression, where interest rate is regressed onto time in years without accounting for which party controls the White House. The low R-squared, adjusted R-squared, F statistic, and Durbin–Watson statistic suggest possible missing explanatory variables or incorrect functional form. The simple linear regression model had a determinant equal to 1 simply because, with only one independent variable, there were no other independent variables to be correlated. We can conclude from this that a straight-line regression is not adequate to capture the movement of the interest rate on 6-month commercial bonds over time.

Polynomial Regression and Perfect Multicollinearity

An obvious nonspline alternative is polynomial regression, where interest rates are regressed onto year, year-squared, year-cubed, et cetera to try to capture the nonlinear movement of interest rates over time. The second row of Table 3.1 presents the results of the polynomial regression. The R-squared, adjusted R-squared, and F statistic are somewhat better than the simple regression, but only three variables were retained. Although independent variables were tried with powers ranging from 1 to 12, nine of these candidates were thrown out because of their perfect correlation with a linear combination of the included independent variables. In fact, only three of the candidates, with powers of 1, 2, and 5 survived. Thus, each of the nine variables thrown out can be exactly represented by a linear combination of year, year-squared, and year raised to the fifth power. Year-cubed and year to the fourth power could not enter the equation because each of them is perfectly correlated with a linear combination of year and year-squared (even without year to the fifth power).

This problem with perfect multicollinearity is one reason that polynomial regressions have not always worked out very well in practice. The three remaining independent variables are not able to do a very good job of capturing the movement of interest rates over time as is evident in the statistics given for the polynomial regression in Table 3.1. Because the determinant that measures the degree of remaining multicollinearity is close to 1 when multicollinearity is low and close to 0 when multicollinearity is high, all of the models except the simple regression model exhibit a high degree of multicollinearity.

F Statistics and *t* Statistics

The high degree of multicollinearity that is evident for most of these models makes it difficult to sort out the relative contributions of the different independent variables in explaining interest rate movements. However, except for the simple regression model, all of these models have F statistics that are strongly statistically significant. Figure 3.3 provided the linear spline model estimation results that show five strongly statistically significant t-statistic interest rate spline adjustments for the five administrations that began in 1920, 1932, 1976, 1980, and 1992. Each of the Republican victories (1920 and 1980) at first appears to have led to a strong downward adjustment to the slope of interest rates with respect to time. In contrast, the Democratic victories (1932, 1976, and 1992) appear to show strong upward adjustments in the slope. This sharp contrast was shown to be misleading in the analysis of the difference in the weighted regression slopes provided earlier.

It is interesting to note that these t statistics are weakened, along with the F statistic for the overall model, with more smoothing in the form of higher order spline regressions (i.e., quadratic, cubic, quartic, and quintic). In other words, we can reject the hypothesis that, in general, Democratic administrations tend to move toward raising interest rates, whereas Republican administrations tend to move in the direction of lowering them.

On the other hand, if we prefer to ask whether a specific administration, regardless of political party, had an impact or not, then the answer is that those five administrations did have significant impacts when we stick with the linear spline model as well as with the cubic spline model. However, most of the other spline models give very mixed results: most of the slope adjustments are statistically insignificant in most models (details not shown).

Autocorrelation and the Durbin–Watson Statistic

In the column labeled "Auto," the Durbin–Watson (DW) statistic fails to reject the null hypothesis of no autocorrelation when the test statistic, DW, is close to 2. Values of DW close to 0 suggest positive autocorrelation, whereas values approaching 4 imply negative autocorrelation. Most of the models have DW values that either reject the null hypothesis in favor of the alternative of positive autocorrelation or are in the indeterminant zone. Only the linear–quadratic–quintic model, which is represented by the last row of Table 3.1, provides a DW statistic sufficiently close to 2. The absence of autocorrelation provides some assurance that this last model has enough structure to represent the data adequately. The linear–quadratic–quintic model also has the highest adjusted R-squared (R-bar-squared), so by that measure, it might be considered the best model. However, even though the R-bar-squared adjusts for degrees of freedom, the estimation of 33 parameters with only 110 observations does limit the confidence level. Even if we accept the overall validity of the model, the very small determinant in the column labeled "Mult," along with the model's weak t statistics (not shown), undermines any attempt to interpret the coefficients of its independent variables. The choice is between a linear spline model, which has a strong F statistic and some good t statistics, and the linear–quadratic–quintic model, which is visually more appealing and has better R-squared, R-bar-squared, and DW statistics, but has a weaker F statistic, t statistics, and multicollinearity measure. The choice really depends on the purpose of performing the estimation to begin with. If we are primarily interested in interpreting the individual coefficients, then the linear spline model may be best. However, if we are interested in the most visually appealing model with the best fit to the data, then the linear–quadratic–quintic model is the best model.

4. SPLINES WITH UNKNOWN KNOT LOCATIONS

In this chapter, we consider the problem of determining the location of spline knots when we are willing to assume that we know how many spline knots there should be, but not exactly where they are located. We also demonstrate that spline regression methods can sometimes be useful with cross-sectional data rather than with only times series data. For a cross-sectional example that uses location instead of time to determine property values, see Marsh and Sindone (1991). In the example that follows, a person's age is used instead of time to determine the strength of his or her commitment to religion.

Our research question comes from the sociology of religion. How does the importance of religion in daily life change over a life cycle? In other words, does a person's age affect the importance of religion to him or her? In particular, if we assume that there are three points in a person's life when the emphasis on the importance of religion in his or her life is altered, at what three ages do these changes occur? How do splines help us determine the appropriate three ages when these changes might take place?

Transforming Discrete Response Into Continuous Measure

The first problem is to formulate an appropriate continuous, interval data measure of the importance of religion in a person's life. To accomplish this, we used data from the 1996 American National Election Survey. We started with the binary response to a survey question that asked, "Is religion an important part of your life?" A total of 1,178 respondents replied "important," whereas 319 said "not important." As a continuous, interval measure, we used the predicted value or estimated probability of responding "important" to this question that was produced by a logistic regression of this binary response onto the responses from a set of other questions that measured religious involvement and commitment.

Specifically, a set of independent variables was used that were transformations of the responses to the following eight questions.

1. How frequently do you pray?
2. How frequently do you read the Bible?
3. Is the Bible the word of God?
4. Do you attend religious services?
5. What is your opinion on the school prayer issue?
6. How strongly do you feel about the school prayer issue?
7. How many church groups are you involved with?
8. How many other religion groups are you involved with?

The predicted values from this logistic regression were concordant with the observed values 93.3% of the time and discordant 6.7%. The likelihood ratio, chi-square test statistic of the overall relevance of this logistic regression was 777.6, which was highly significant with a p value of less than .0001. Simply put, the eight questions did a good job of explaining the importance of religion in people's lives. This result enabled us to use the predicted values from this logistic regression as a continuous, interval measure of the importance of religion as it relates to a person's age in a spline regression model. Of course, it is important to point out that because we are using only a cross-sectional data set, we cannot separate out the effect of age from cohort effects. Consequently, "age" could just as easily be replaced with "year of birth" and all the age effects could be attributed to generational differences. Moreover, the reader may find other measures of religiosity more compelling such as it is in Leege and Kellstedt (1993) or Leege, Kellstedt, and Wald (1990).

Before running any regressions to explain the importance of religion, we first plotted the predicted measure of religion's importance against age as shown in Figure 4.1 to get an overview of the data. Ages below 20 and above 76 tended to represent less than 10 persons,

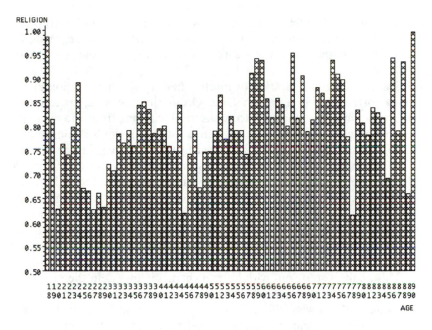

Figure 4.1. Predicted Importance of Religion Versus Age

so their values for the predicted importance of religion are likely to be less reliable and more extreme than an average over a larger group of persons. This fact accounts for the large incremental differences in the predicted importance of religion at either end of the age spectrum.

Interrupted Regression Analysis

Intervention or interrupted regression methods have been better explained and more widely used than spline regression methods. For example, see the discussion by Lewis-Beck (1986) concerning the impact of the Cuban revolution on Cuban economic growth, the effect of various coal mine safety laws on coal mine fatalities, and how traffic fatalities in Kentucky responded to a change in the speed limit. Consequently, it is useful at this point to present the basic problem of relating the importance of religion to a person's age in terms of a version of intervention or interrupted regression analysis. Note that the essential difference between intervention/interrupted regressions and spline regressions is that intervention/interrupted regressions emphasize abrupt changes, whereas spline regressions focus on smoother transitions with no visible breaks in the regression line.

The fundamental question of interest here is whether religion plays an important role in a person's life. Ordinarily, the constant term or intercept shifts the question to measure deviations from the average role of religion. However, we want to know if a person's commitment is different from 0, not if it is different from the average commitment. Consequently, the constant term must be included with the independent variables to explain the extent of one's commitment as it deviates from 0 to ensure that the R-squared and F statistic in the regression answer the appropriate question. The regressions in this chapter are designed to provide both a measure of how one's commitment to religion deviates from 0 as well as an overall test of the statistical significance of that measure.

This analysis starts out with known change points as in the previous chapter, but then switches to variable change points to demonstrate the effect of allowing the change points or spline knots to be estimated from the sample data. The analysis begins with a simple version of intervention/interrupted regression analysis with change points located at ages 35 ($K1 = 35$), 55 ($K2 = 55$), and 75 ($K3 = 75$). We assume that these change points are justified either on the basis of theoretical analysis or from past empirical studies.

Adjusting Intercepts Only

The first intervention/interrupted regression allows only for shifts in the regression line at each of the three prespecified change points. To accomplish this, we need to define three dummy variables that correspond to the change points at ages $K1 = 35$, $K2 = 55$, and $K3 = 75$. Therefore, the first dummy variable is 0 ($D1 = 0$) for all persons less than or equal to $K1$ years of age and is 1 ($D1 = 1$) for anyone older than $K1$. The second dummy variable is 0 ($D2 = 0$) for ages less than or equal to $K2$ and equal to 1 ($D2 = 1$) for ages greater than $K2$. Similarly, the third dummy variable is 0 ($D3 = 0$) for ages $K3$ or less and equal to 1 ($D3 = 1$) for ages over $K3$.

Figure 4.2a presents the results of regressing our measure of the importance of religion on age and three adjustments in the form of shifts in the regression line at ages 35 ($K1 = 35$), 55 ($K2 = 55$),

```
Dependent Variable: RELIGION

Analysis of Variance

                        Sum of          Mean
Source          DF      Squares         Square      F Value     Prob>F

Model            5      930.03890     186.00778     2146.879    0.0001
Error         1492      129.26842       0.08664
U Total       1497     1059.30732


        Root MSE        0.29435     R-square       0.8780
        Dep Mean        0.78690     Adj R-sq       0.8776
        C.V.           37.40594

Parameter Estimates

                    Parameter     Standard     T for H0:
Variable   DF       Estimate         Error    Parameter=0    Prob > |T|

INTERCEPT   1       0.737548    0.04373969        16.862     0.0001
AGE         1      -0.000294    0.00142988        -0.206     0.8369
D1          1       0.056538    0.02898770         1.950     0.0513
D2          1       0.076162    0.03561182         2.139     0.0326
D3          1      -0.029216    0.03873475        -0.754     0.4508
```

(a)

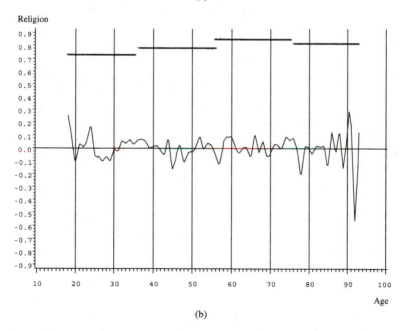

(b)

Figure 4.2. Religion Importance (a) With Dummy Variable Shifts and (b) With Shifts and Plot of Residuals

and 75 ($K3 = 75$). The overall fit is good with an R-squared value of 0.8780 and an F-statistic value of 2146.879. This result is highly significant in rejecting the null hypothesis that age is not important in explaining why religious importance is not 0. However, the coefficient and t statistic associated with the age variable show that age does not affect religious commitment in a continuous manner. Instead, age affects religious commitment through three discrete shifts in the regression line. In particular, the regression line shifts upward while staying parallel to the original line at age 35 and again at age 55, and then shifts downward at age 75, which ages correspond to the dummy variables $D1$, $D2$, and $D3$ with coefficients 0.056538, 0.076162, and −0.029216, respectively. However, only the first two of these estimated coefficients are anywhere near being statistically significant. The three shifts can be seen in Figure 4.2b, which displays the predicted regression line (broken into three parts) and a plot of the regression residuals (the jagged line around 0).

The immediate impression from looking at the predicted regression line is that there is too much rigid structure and not enough flexibility to adequately represent behavior that might be explained on a more intuitive level. In particular, forcing the lines to be parallel seems to be unwarranted as is suggested by the residual plot. If these data were time series, the residual pattern would suggest a strong positive autocorrelation because the residuals are slow to cross the 0 line. However, not only are the residuals slow to cross 0, but they exhibit a downward drift that corresponds to the upward slope of each of the regression line segments. This is a clear tipoff that the model is misspecified and too rigid to really represent what is going on here.

Adjusting Intercepts and Slopes

Consequently, we now try a more flexible approach to intervention/interrupted regression analysis. Additional flexibility can be introduced by allowing the slopes of the lines as well as their intercepts to adjust at each of the change points. This is accomplished by introducing three more independent variables into our regression. Each of the three new variables corresponds to each of the original dummy variables multiplied by the variable age. Multiplying age by a dummy variable introduces an adjustment to the slope of the regression line at the same time that the line is shifted by the corresponding original dummy variable term. In other words, the dummy variables, $D1$, $D2$, and $D3$ will shift the regression line at the same time as $D1^*$age, $D2^*$age, and $D3^*$age adjust the slope of the regression line.

The results of running this second intervention/interrupted regression can be seen in Figure 4.3a. The R-squared of .8783 and corresponding F statistic of 1342.726 with a p value of less than .0001 present clear evidence of the model's ability to explain deviations from a world where religion was perceived to be of no importance in people's lives. In other words, the overall model of age with dummy variable shifts and slope adjustments does a good job of explaining the deviations of the measure of the importance of religion from a base of 0 importance. However, the variable age has an estimated coefficient value of 0.002402 with a t statistic of 0.789 and p value of .4300, so it is clearly not statistically significantly different from 0. In fact, the only statistically significant coefficient estimate is the one for shifting the regression line at age 35.

As can be seen in Figure 4.3b, the slope with respect to age shifts from a positive value of 0.002402 to a negative value of -0.003300 (which is 0.002402 minus 0.005702). The regression line, which was upward sloping prior to age 35, is now slightly downward sloping after age 35. The regression line also shifts upward by 0.267513 as measured along the vertical axis at age 35. Because an age of 0 is outside the relevant range of our sample data, the amount of upward shift is statistically important for model flexibility, but does not lend itself to meaningful, intuitive interpretation. The third and fourth regression line segments shown in Figure 4.3b are not statistically, significantly different from the second line segment, because their t statistics are too small and their p values are too large to be of importance here.

Splines With Known Knot Locations

Spline models are appropriate when changes are not abrupt but are more of a change in direction. This means that spline models do not allow for breaks in the regression line, only for changes in slope or more subtle changes. The emphasis with splines is on smoothing, so dramatic changes are not appropriate for splines. However, in the current context, a change in attitude toward religion might occur gradually after reaching certain ages, so a spline model might be useful here.

The first spline model has fixed spline knots at ages $K1 = 35$, $K2 = 55$, and $K3 = 75$. Later on, we allow $K1$, $K2$, and $K3$ to

```
Dependent Variable: RELIGION

Analysis of Variance

                        Sum of          Mean
      Source      DF    Squares         Square     F Value      Prob>F

      Model        8    930.34540    116.29317    1342.726      0.0001
      Error     1489    128.96192      0.08661
      U Total   1497   1059.30732


           Root MSE        0.29430    R-square      0.8783
           Dep Mean        0.78690    Adj R-sq      0.8776
           C.V.           37.39919

Parameter Estimates

                      Parameter      Standard    T for H0:
      Variable   DF   Estimate        Error     Parameter=0    Prob > |T|

      INTERCEPT   1    0.659650     0.08908126      7.405        0.0001
      AGE         1    0.002402     0.00304345      0.789        0.4300
      D1          1    0.267513     0.13154588      2.034        0.0422
      D2          1   -0.214792     0.19886445     -1.080        0.2803
      D3          1    0.114707     0.52637577      0.218        0.8275
      D1*AGE      1   -0.005702     0.00373687     -1.526        0.1273
      D2*AGE      1    0.005429     0.00342944      1.583        0.1136
      D3*AGE      1   -0.002253     0.00664350     -0.339        0.7346
```

(a)

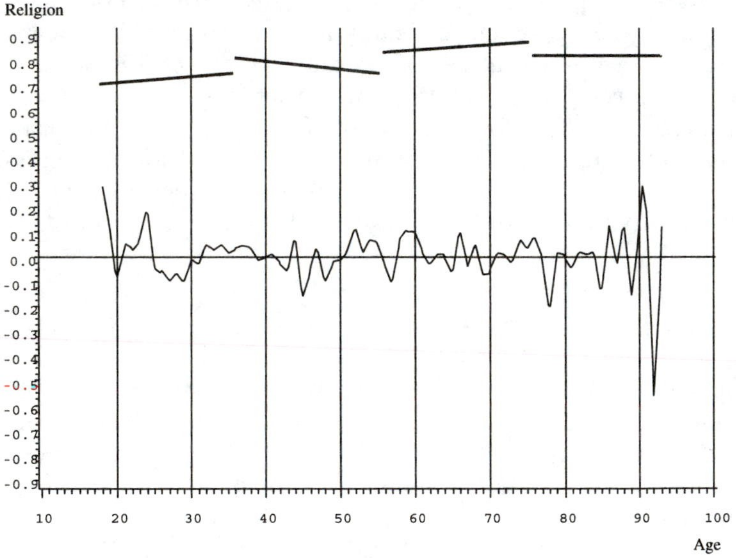

(b)

Figure 4.3. (a) Dummy Variable Shifts and Slope Adjustments, and (b) Shifts, Changing Slopes, and Plot of Residuals

be unknown parameters to be estimated, but for now they are fixed. For details on how to estimate unknown spline knots such as $K1$, $K2$, and $K3$, see Marsh, Maudgal, and Raman (1990). We can now use the same dummy variables specified previously to create three new variables that will serve as independent variables for the spline regression. These three new variables are defined as $D1^*(\text{age} - K1)$, $D2^*(\text{age} - K2)$, and $D3^*(\text{age} - K3)$. Remember that we defined $D1$ to be 0 until age passes $K1$, after which $D1$ becomes equal to 1. This means that $D1^*(\text{age} - K1)$ can never be negative, that it is initially 0, and takes on values $1, 2, 3, \ldots$ as age exceeds $K1$ by $1, 2, 3, \ldots$ years. Analogous structures exist for $D2^*(\text{age} - K2)$ and $D3^*(\text{age} - K3)$. In all, this spline model has only four independent variables: age, $D1^*(\text{age} - K1)$, $D2^*(\text{age} - K2)$, and $D3^*(\text{age} - K3)$. Figure 4.4a displays the results of running the spline regression with these four explanatory variables.

The regression results in Figure 4.4a show a slight reduction in the R-squared value from .8783 in the last regression to .8776. However, the last regression had three more parameters and, therefore, used up 3 more degrees of freedom. Moreover, the F statistic for testing the significance of the regression as a whole has increased from 1342.726 to 2138.596 for this spline regression. Also, the age variable itself has a statistically significant coefficient with a t statistic of 2.040 and a corresponding p value of .0416.

Ultimately, we should look to theory, at least in the form of commonsense intuition, to guide us in choosing the appropriate regression model. If we are uncomfortable with the abrupt jumps in the importance of religion at particular ages, then we might prefer the spline model because there are no jumps in the function, only an adjustment to the line's slope at each of the three spline knots. Before age 35, the importance of religion increases with age along a rising straight line with a positive slope of 0.005082. After age 35 the slope changes to a smaller positive value of 0.001222 (i.e., 0.005082 minus 0.003860). This can be seen in Figure 4.4b, where the positively sloped regression line pivots at age 35 to produce a less positively sloped regression line to the right of age 35.

The next change takes place at age 55. To the left of age 55 the regression line has a slight positive slope of 0.001222, which at age 55 changes to a positive slope of 0.003932 (i.e., 0.001222 plus 0.002710). Again, this can be seen as the positively sloped line in Figure 4.4b from age 55 to age 75. Finally, at age 75, the regression pivots

Dependent Variable: RELIGION

Analysis of Variance

Source	DF	Sum of Squares	Mean Square	F Value	Prob>F
Model	5	929.59954	185.91991	2138.596	0.0001
Error	1492	129.70778	0.08694		
U Total	1497	1059.30732			

Root MSE	0.29485	R-square	0.8776
Dep Mean	0.78690	Adj R-sq	0.8771
C.V.	37.46946		

Parameter Estimates

Variable	DF	Parameter Estimate	Standard Error	T for H0: Parameter=0	Prob > |T|
INTERCEPT	1	0.592060	0.07745123	7.644	0.0001
AGE	1	0.005082	0.00249142	2.040	0.0416
D1*(AGE-K1)	1	-0.003860	0.00344656	-1.120	0.2629
D2*(AGE-K2)	1	0.002710	0.00286049	0.947	0.3436
D3*(AGE-K3)	1	-0.009868	0.00536717	-1.839	0.0662

(a)

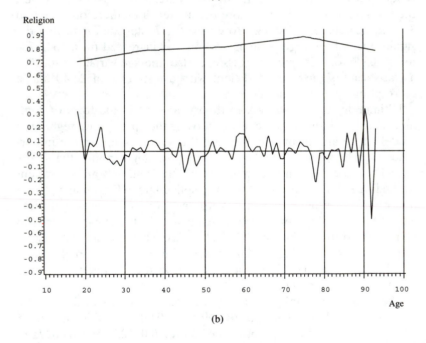

(b)

Figure 4.4. (a) Regression With Three Spline Knot Adjustments and (b) Three Spline Knots and Plot of Residuals

downward with a negative slope of −0.005936 (i.e., 0.003932 minus 0.009868). The residual plot around zero in Figure 4.4b is fairly well behaved, although it does retain its relatively large variances (i.e., heteroskedasticity) at either end of the age spectrum, which simply may be due to the shortage of observations near the end points.

The end result of all these twists and turns is a rather reasonable looking predicted regression line that depicts our measure of the importance of religion in people's lives. More specifically, according to our spline regression as depicted in Figure 4.4b, the importance of religion increases until age 35. Perhaps families who are raising children increase their emphasis on religious values as their children pass through their formative years. In any case, after age 35 there is a more gradual increase in the importance of religion until age 55 is reached, when religion rises more sharply in importance. Perhaps there is a revival in interest in religion as the retirement years approach. Finally, after age 75 there seems to be a gradual decrease in religion's importance, which is difficult to explain.

Unknown Spline Knot Location Estimation

We must now face up to the rather arbitrary assumption we have made about the location of the change points or spline knots, and address the key point of this chapter, which is to demonstrate how to estimate the location of these spline knots. In particular, we have treated $K1$, $K2$, and $K3$ as known constants, but now we wish to estimate them along with the usual regression coefficients in our spline model. To do this, we must switch to nonlinear least squares regression, because there will be terms in our model that involve the product of these spline knot parameters and the usual regression coefficients. These terms are essentially cross-product terms from the interaction between the spline knot parameters and the regression coefficients. The model we now wish to estimate can be expressed as

$$Y_i = a + b0^* \text{ age}_i + b1^* D1_i^* (\text{age}_i - K1) + b2^* D2_i^* (\text{age}_i - K2)$$
$$+ b3^* D3_i^* (\text{age}_i - K3) + e_i, \tag{4.1}$$

where Y_i is our measure of the importance of religion and e_i is the error term for the ith individual. Equation 4.1 can be rewritten more appropriately for nonlinear estimation as

$$Y_i = a + b0^* \text{ age}_i + b1^* D1_i^* \text{ age}_i - b1^* K1^* D1_i + b2^* D2_i^* \text{ age}_i$$
$$- b2^* K2^* D2_i + b3^* D3_i^* \text{ age}_i - b3^* K3^* D3_i + e_i.$$

Notice the three cross-product terms $b1^* K1$, $b2^* K2$, and $b3^* K3$. These cross-product terms require that we use nonlinear regression methods to estimate the eight regression parameters a, $b0$, $b1$, $K1$, $b2$, $K2$, $b3$, and $K3$.

After eight iterations, the nonlinear least squares procedure successfully converged to the spline regression results presented in Figure 4.5a. The ratio of the explained mean squares to the unexplained (i.e., residual) mean squares of 1341.427 is substantial, although it does not have an F distribution due to the nonlinear nature of the model. The asymptotic 95% confidence intervals reveal that six of the estimated regression parameters are statistically significant asymptotically at the 5% level of significance or better. For details on how to properly interpret the estimated coefficients of a nonlinear model, see Marsh, McGlynn, and Chakraborty (1994). More interestingly, we see that the original spline knot locations of 35, 55, and 75 have now been replaced with values of approximately 38, 45, and 71. Although we have maintained the assumption that there are three and only three such knot locations, we have added considerable flexibility in allowing the regression procedure to estimate the locations of these three spline knots.

Figure 4.5b shows the plot of the predicted importance of religion and the corresponding regression residuals. The shape of the resulting predicted regression line for the importance of religion tells a story similar to that for the fixed-knot locations except that the change points or spline knots have been changed and the slopes of the lines have been adjusted slightly to accommodate this fact. Using exactly the same procedure to calculate the slopes of the four regression line segments as in the previous fixed-knot spline regression, we calculate the four slopes to be 0.006600, −0.008731, 0.005166, and −0.004458. In a sense, this result confirms the general conclusion of the previous three regressions, but with somewhat more flexibility in estimation and, therefore, in a more convincing manner.

```
Nonlinear Least Squares                 Dependent Variable RELIGION

Source              DF Sum of Squares    Mean Square

Regression           8     930.2356945   116.2794618
Residual          1489     129.0716244     0.0866834
Uncorrected Total 1497    1059.3073190

(Corrected Total) 1496     132.3403831


Parameter    Estimate      Asymptotic                 Asymptotic 95 %
                           Std. Error             Confidence Interval

                                                  Lower          Upper
a          0.55023847   0.0733452077    0.406365054    0.694111883
b0         0.00660004   0.0023532240    0.001983975    0.011216108
b1        -0.01533073   0.0102628071   -0.035462174    0.004800718
b2         0.01389691   0.0101348790   -0.005983597    0.033777409
b3        -0.00962422   0.0041393418   -0.017743920   -0.001504515
K1        38.34476292   3.0079866802   32.444318602   44.245207241
K2        45.00016922   3.1670657405   38.787676594   51.212661838
K3        70.93992636   4.4706774525   62.170278687   79.709574026
```

(a)

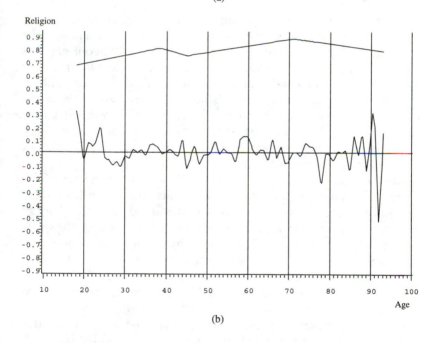

(b)

Figure 4.5. (a) "Linear" Nonlinear Spline Regression Output and (b) "Linear" Nonlinear Spline and Residual Plot

Quadratic Spline With Unknown Knot Locations

Finally, we would like to add quadratic terms to our spline regression to see if the strictly straight-line shape of our line segments is still too restrictive even with the flexible spline knots. Is there value to be gained by moving from a linear spline model to a quadratic spline model? We now add some quadratic terms to our spline model, estimate it, and then view the results to see if our model is significantly improved. The following three quadratic variables are needed to expand our flexible spline regression model: $D1^*(\text{age} - K1)^2$, $D2^*(\text{age} - K2)^2$, and $D3^*(\text{age} - K3)^2$. The following quadratic expression are now added to Equation 4.1:

$$+ c1^*D1^*(\text{age} - K1)^2 + c2^*D2^*(\text{age} - K2)^2 + c3^*D3^*(\text{age} - K3)^2.$$

We now have 11 parameters to estimate: $a, b0, b1, c1, K1, b2, c2, K2, b3, c3,$ and $K3$.

Figure 4.6a presents the results of our nonlinear least squares regression, which successfully converged after 17 iterations. The mean square ratio has fallen from a value of 1341.427 in our previous nonlinear regression to 976.387, which largely reflects the fact that we have added three additional parameters to our model without substantially increasing the model's fit to the data. As in the previous nonlinear spline regression, six of the parameter estimates were statistically significant at least at the 5% level or better. However, the three additional parameters, $c1, c2,$ and $c3$, are not significantly different from 0 asymptotically at the 5% level.

Another interesting aspect of Figure 4.6a is the estimates of the three spline knot locations. Here we see that the spline knots have shifted once again and are now located at 38.8, 45, and 75. Although we introduced even more flexiblity with the quadratic terms, the spline knot estimates have not changed much from the previous nonlinear estimates of 38, 45, and 71. This just goes to show that it is hard to anticipate the outcome of estimating nonlinear models, especially because they tend to be more unstable mathematically than linear ones, except in very simple, well-behaved situations.

Figure 4.6b presents the graph of our quadratic spline model that predicts the importance of religion as well as the model's residuals plotted around 0. The residuals have not changed much and still show rather high variance at the extreme ends. The predicted measure of

```
Nonlinear Least Squares                    Dependent Variable RELIGION

Source                 DF Sum of Squares      Mean Square

Regression             11      930.5572680    84.5961153
Residual             1486      128.7500509     0.0866420
Uncorrected Total    1497     1059.3073190

(Corrected Total)    1496      132.3403831
```

Parameter	Estimate	Asymptotic Std. Error	Asymptotic 95 % Confidence Interval	
			Lower	Upper
a	0.54426795	0.0733276900	0.400428663	0.688107238
b0	0.00683247	0.0023526620	0.002217493	0.011447437
b1	-0.02042923	0.0380162369	-0.095001721	0.054143259
b2	0.02573383	0.0363784842	-0.045626050	0.097093712
b3	-0.01467719	0.0173492795	-0.048709466	0.019355081
K1	38.76809688	2.7736059078	33.327403213	44.208790539
K2	45.01350018	2.2833322824	40.534525198	49.492475168
K3	75.00005679	5.2503427827	64.701006504	85.299107067
c1	-0.00010227	0.0056382248	-0.011162184	0.010957652
c2	-0.00010365	0.0056410996	-0.011169208	0.010961907
c3	0.00124009	0.0013750718	-0.001457248	0.003937422

(a)

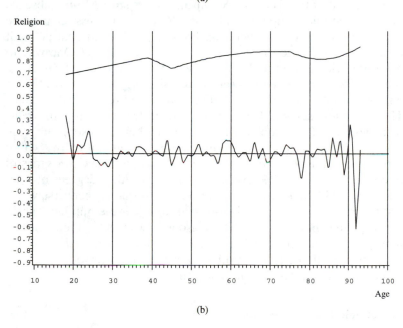

(b)

Figure 4.6. (a) "Quadratic" Nonlinear Spline Regression Output and (b) "Quadratic" Nonlinear Spline and Residual Plot

religion's importance displays a dip in its last segment that was not available with the strictly linear spline segments estimated previously. The minimum point of the dip in the last segment can be calculated mathematically from the nonlinear regression estimates by solving the equation

$$\text{age} = \frac{[b0 + (b1 - 2^*K1^*c1) + (b2 - 2^*K2^*c2) + (b3 - 2^*K3^*c3)]}{[-2^*(c1 + c2 + c3)]}.$$

These calculations produce the solution age = 82.81657513. These results suggest that the importance of religion increases until it peaks at 38.8 years of age, then dips down to a local minimum at about age 45, then rises to another peak at about 75, then dips to another local minimum at 82.8, and rises thereafter.

The Wald Test

At the end of the day, how convincing is this story? In the absence of any theoretical support, this last nonlinear regression may be too precise to be very convincing. From a purely statistical point of view, can this charge of spurious precision be upheld? One way to determine this is with a Wald test, which tests the set of quadratic coefficients $c1, c2$, and $c3$ to see if, as a set, they are statistically significant or not. The Wald test statistic value for this test is 0.5755006. The Wald test statistic has a chi-square distribution asymptotically with degrees of freedom equal to the number of restrictions (see Greene, 2000). Whereas the null hypothesis consists of the set of three restrictions, $c1 = 0$, $c2 = 0$, and $c3 = 0$, we have 3 degrees of freedom. Even at a 10% level of significance with 3 degrees of freedom, the table chi-square value of 6.25 is too large; conversely, the test statistic value of 0.5755 is too small to reject the null hypothesis. Consequently, both for statistical reasons as well as for the common-sense, "spurious precision" argument already mentioned, we must reject this quadratic spline model in favor of the previous nonlinear model, which was our "linear" spline model.

Model Selection Conclusion

We have answered our research question about how and to what extent the importance of religion changes over a person's life cycle with estimation and testing in the context of spline regression models. Our best model was the "linear" nonlinear spline model, which allowed the nonlinear least squares estimation procedure to determine the location of the three spline knots. We conclude that people perceive that religion plays an important role in their life cycle with a rise in reported importance reaching an initial peak at age 38, then a drop in importance until age 45, followed by a rise in importance until 71, where it peaks again and drops off slowly from there.

It is important to emphasize, however, that our failure to control for cohort effects and other appropriate control variables means that this exercise provides a suggested methodology rather than a definitive research conclusion for this problem.

5. SPLINES WITH AN UNKNOWN NUMBER OF KNOTS

In the previous chapters, we assumed that we knew the exact number of spline knots in advance. When we also knew the location of those spline knots, we had a restricted, linear least squares problem. When we did not know the location of the spline knots, the spline knots became additional parameters that had to be estimated along with the regression coefficients (which are also parameters), so the problem became a nonlinear least squares problem. In this chapter, the problem becomes even more complicated in that we do not even know the number of spline knots. The method of estimation used in this example was first proposed by Marsh (1983) and then revised and republished (Marsh, 1986). We use time measured in number of days as the spline variable (an independent variable).

Stepwise Regression as a Powerful Nonparametric Method

Our general strategy for dealing with this problem is to create a large number of potential spline knots and then use stepwise regression to pick out those that are most statistically significant. In stepwise regression, we do not know a priori which variables or even how many variables ultimately will be chosen. Whereas we do not know the number of variables, we do not know the number of coefficients (i.e., parameters) that the model ultimately will require. When the number of parameters is not known in advance of estimation, the estimation method is called a nonparametric method. In a sense, this term is ironic in that a model estimated nonparametrically (i.e., a nonparametric model) typically ends up having a lot more parameters than a model estimated parametrically. In other words, by definition, the number of parameters (and functional form) in a parametric model is known in advance of estimation, whereas the number of parameters (or functional form) in a nonparametric model is not known in advance.

To motivate this chapter, we have chosen a research problem related to your financial well-being in retirement. In particular, we are interested in the problem of how to estimate the growth of your TIAA–CREF retirement account. In other words, this chapter will focuses on estimation, per se, rather than on hypothesis testing issues, especially given the difficulty in determining proper statistical distributions in this context. Figure 5.1 displays a representation of the screen you see at the TIAA–CREF web site that allows you to reallocate your retirement account premiums. A similar screen allows

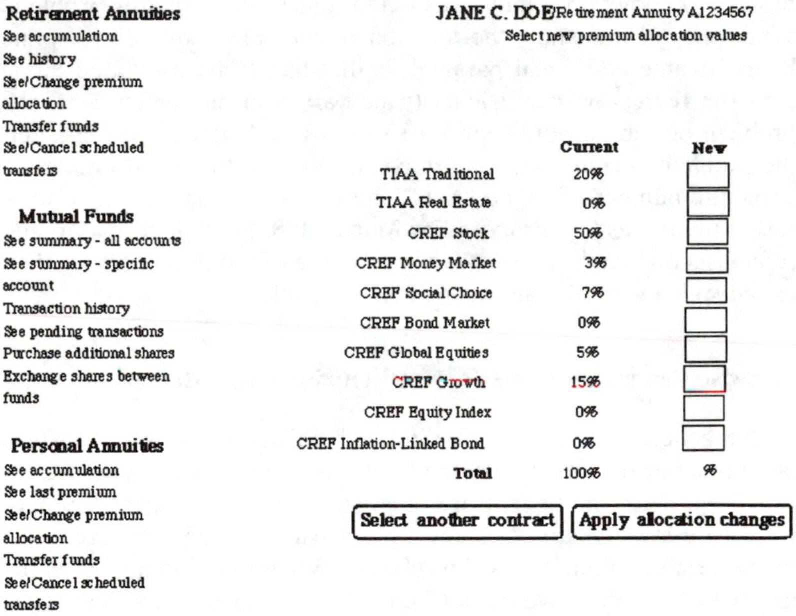

Retirement Annuities

See accumulation
See history
See/Change premium allocation
Transfer funds
See/Cancel scheduled transfers

Mutual Funds

See summary - all accounts
See summary - specific account
Transaction history
See pending transactions
Purchase additional shares
Exchange shares between funds

Personal Annuities

See accumulation
See last premium
See/Change premium allocation
Transfer funds
See/Cancel scheduled transfers

JANE C. DOE/Retirement Annuity A1234567
Select new premium allocation values

	Current	New
TIAA Traditional	20%	☐
TIAA Real Estate	0%	☐
CREF Stock	50%	☐
CREF Money Market	3%	☐
CREF Social Choice	7%	☐
CREF Bond Market	0%	☐
CREF Global Equities	5%	☐
CREF Growth	15%	☐
CREF Equity Index	0%	☐
CREF Inflation-Linked Bond	0%	☐
Total	**100%**	**%**

[**Select another contract**] [**Apply allocation changes**]

Figure 5.1. TIAA–CREF Retirement Account Reallocation Screen

you to reallocate your principal, but the principal may not be reallocated more than three times a month (i.e., TIAA–CREF does not allow "day trading"). As of June 30, 2000 the largest account was the CREF Stock account with $133.0 billion, followed by CREF Growth with $17.2 billion, CREF Global Equities with $9.7 billion, CREF Money Market with $6.6 billion, and so forth. The point is that the CREF Stock account contains by far the largest portion of the retirement money. Consequently, we use the CREF Stock account unit value (i.e., price per share) to demonstrate our method of searching for the number and location of spline knots and, therefore, obtaining a good representation of the rate of growth of the most important TIAA–CREF retirement account.

The immediately available data for the CREF Stock account range from April 1, 1988 to the present. Figure 5.2 displays a graph of the last three years of these data. Initially we use only the data for the years 1998, 1999, and 2000 to estimate our spline regression model. Later on, toward the end of this chapter, we briefly mention the problem of out-of-sample forecasting, where we estimate with the data from 1988 to 1998 and then forecast for the years 1999 and 2000.

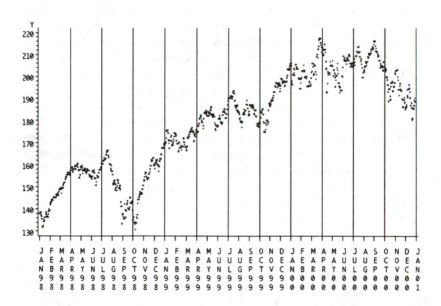

Figure 5.2. CREF Stock Account Values for 1998, 1999, and 2000

Naturally, it is a lot easier to represent what has happened in the past than to forecast the future. However, it is useful to get a sense of the limitations of this technology.

Determining the Number, Location, and Degree of the Spline Knots

First we must decide how smooth we want the spline fit to be. In other words, do we want to use linear spline knots, quadratic spline knots, cubic knots, or what? In this case, we use cubic knots, although we could throw in several different types of knots and let the stepwise regression select the most appropriate. We do not know the number of knots that ultimately will be chosen by the stepwise regression, but we do have to set up a fixed set of potential knots to be considered. One way to set up the spline knots is first to break the observed range of the data into a large number of equal intervals. By definition, the intervals must be separated by a corresponding set of grid values, which, in this case, are measured as the day number or, in effect, the observation number for these time-ordered data. An alternative approach is to use the observed values of the spline variable as the potential knot locations. When time data are used, often there may be no difference between these two approaches. However, in cross-sectional data such as the spline variable "age" in the religion–age example in the previous chapter, a grid of prespecified age values may include ages that are not directly observed in the data. Moreover, if time is measured in integer values like years, a prespecified grid could even be expressed in fractions of a year (e.g., quarters, months, weeks, etc.) so that a change can occur part way through a year.

Whereas we have 772 observations for the CREF Stock data, we first create 772 dummy variables where D_j equals 1 if TIME is greater than K_j; otherwise, D_j equals 0, where $K_j = j$, for $j = 1, \ldots, 772$. Next, we set up 772 cubic spline knot variables, defined as $C_j = D_j^*(\text{TIME} - K_j)^3$, where $j = 1, \ldots, 772$. Note that $K_1 = 1$ for every observation, $K_2 = 2$ for every observation, and so forth. For example, $K_{250} = 250$ for every observation, whereas $D_{250} = 0$ when TIME is less than or equal to 250 and $D_{250} = 1$ when TIME is greater than 250. Consequently, $C_{250} = $ zero for observations 1 through 250, but $C_{250} = 1$, $C_{250} = 2$, $C_{250} = 3$, et cetera for observations 251, 252, 253, et cetera, respectively. All of the 772 cubic spline knot adjustment variables from C_1 through C_{772} are constructed in this same manner.

Of course, the stepwise regression will select only a statistically significant subset of these 772 variables to actually enter our CREF Stock model.

Our stepwise regression has the CREF Stock unit value as the dependent variable. The independent variables include TIME, which was given as the number of days since January 1, 1960 (even though our data do not begin until April 1, 1988). We also use TIME-squared and TIME-cubed as potential independent variables, in addition to the 772 cubic spline variables. The stepwise regression procedure generates a large number of steps, where it adds (subtracts) a variable to (from) the model at each step. To illustrate the problem of deciding which step represents the best model for our purpose, we compare the output and corresponding graphs for steps 7, 19, and 51.

Smooth Splines for Long-Term Investing

Step 7 is interesting because it is the step that maximizes the F statistic for overall significance of the model and has an R-squared greater than .95, so it explains more than 95% of the variation in the unit value of the CREF Stock as can be seen in Figure 5.3. Amazingly enough, it does all this with only five cubic spline knots. The five spline knots are designated $C2$, $C155$, $C201$, $C207$, and $C457$, and correspond to observation numbers 2, 155, 201, 207, and 457, respectively. Even though the stepwise procedure did not choose TIME-cubed to enter the model, the fact that $C2$ entered means that a cubic term was needed already at the second observation. The column labeled "F" is the square of the corresponding t statistics with p values in the last column being exactly the same for the one-sided F test and the corresponding two-sided t test. The significance level to enter (SLE) the model and the significance level to stay (SLS) in the model were set very leniently at values close to 1 to make it easy for variables to enter and stay in the model. However, whereas the purpose of the model is to represent the performance of the CREF Stock, Figure 5.4 presents a graph of the fitted or predicted unit values as the line among the observed unit value points on the graph.

As an overall representation of CREF Stock performance from a long-term perspective, the model does fairly well. In particular, the graph shows that the general trend has been upward with a somewhat dramatic move downward in the late summer and early fall of 1998 and, more recently, with a downward slide from July 2000 onward.

Step 7   Variable C155 Entered   R-square = 0.95650149   C(p) =2566.6190888

	DF	Sum of Squares	Mean Square	F	Prob>F
Regression	7	370543.15870787	52934.73695827	2399.97	0.0001
Error	764	16851.07033340	22.05637478		
Total	771	387394.22904127			

Variable	Parameter Estimate	Standard Error	Type II Sum of Squares	F	Prob>F
INTERCEP	-80052.36051336	71047.44191595	28.00177273	1.27	0.2602
TIME	11.26320253	10.19385500	26.92656880	1.22	0.2696
TIME2	-0.00039526	0.00036565	25.77235991	1.17	0.2801
C2	-0.00000262	0.00000089	189.79815644	8.61	0.0035
C155	0.00006566	0.00000427	5215.85890751	236.48	0.0001
C201	-0.00053396	0.00002441	10557.43367619	478.66	0.0001
C207	0.00047229	0.00002105	11103.95419105	503.44	0.0001
C457	-0.00000253	0.00000011	11177.16662288	506.75	0.0001

Bounds on condition number: 4.3633E8,   1.069E10

Figure 5.3. Stepwise Regression Output for Step 7

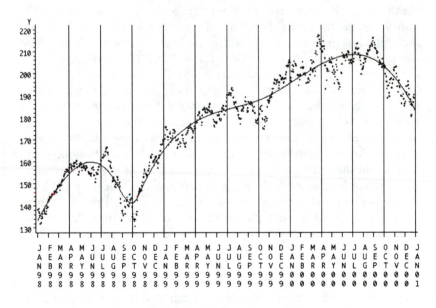

Figure 5.4. Graph of Actual/Predicted CREF Stock Values at Step 7

This representation may be adequate for younger people who do not expect to withdraw their money anytime soon, but may not be adequate for older people nearing retirement who need a more precise representation of the general volatility to better assess the short-term risks in the CREF Stock. With this in mind we now move on to step 19.

Moderately Sensitive Splines for Medium-Term Investing

The output for step 19 is presented in Figure 5.5. Although the F statistic is somewhat less than that in step 7, the R-squared is now over .97 and all the regression coefficients are highly statistically significant. There are now 13 spline adjustment variables in the model. Notice that the coefficients alternate in sign. This just means that both upward and downward movements have a tendency to go too

```
Step19   Variable C725 Removed      R-square = 0.97242481   C(p) =1366.3221770

                  DF        Sum of Squares      Mean Square        F     Prob>F

Regression        15      376711.75771329    25114.11718089    1777.33   0.0001
Error            756       10682.47132798       14.13025308
Total            771      387394.22904127

               Parameter          Standard           Type II
Variable        Estimate             Error      Sum of Squares        F     Prob>F

INTERCEP   -623421.7479295  113722.46540764     424.64039460      30.05   0.0001
TIME          89.33933104       16.33327182     422.75519521      29.92   0.0001
TIME2         -0.00319992        0.00058646     420.67664910      29.77   0.0001
C2             0.00000765        0.00000192     223.31994128      15.80   0.0001
C112          -0.00004463        0.00000619     735.65948628      52.06   0.0001
C155           0.00016911        0.00001136    3130.21324889     221.53   0.0001
C201          -0.00114305        0.00005599    5888.84595266     416.75   0.0001
C207           0.00102645        0.00005014    5923.02739335     419.17   0.0001
C298          -0.00002259        0.00000176    2323.76021492     164.45   0.0001
C410           0.00005021        0.00000336    3158.29606936     223.51   0.0001
C457          -0.00012673        0.00000891    2857.81194196     202.25   0.0001
C495           0.00015714        0.00001372    1852.50696608     131.10   0.0001
C537          -0.00018747        0.00001979    1268.27084821      89.76   0.0001
C565           0.00019104        0.00001950    1355.91402697      95.96   0.0001
C615          -0.00028855        0.00002697    1618.06971564     114.51   0.0001
C626           0.00021847        0.00002077    1562.71685288     110.59   0.0001

Bounds on condition number:    3.5848E9,      1.458E11
```

Figure 5.5. Stepwise Regression Output for Step 19

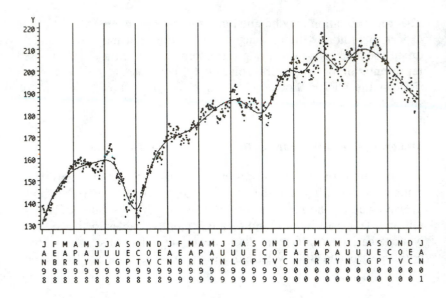

Figure 5.6. Graph of Actual/Predicted CREF Stock Values at Step 19

far if not held in check. This tendency can complicate the problem of forecasting with spline models beyond the scope of the original data. In other words, simple spline models are adequate for interpolating within the domain of the independent variable values, whereas more sophisticated spline models are needed to accurately forecast outside that domain.

Our predicted regression curve is presented among the actual CREF Stock unit values in the graph displayed in Figure 5.6. This graph shows considerably more sensitivity to the data and, therefore, greater flexibility than the graph that represented step 7. Although both pick up the dip in the second half of 1998 and the slide in the second half of 2000, the step 19 graph also detects a dip in the fall of 1999 and the two significant declines in the first half of 2000.

Highly Sensitive Splines for Short-Term Investing

Finally, we move on to step 51, which was our best result prior to automatic termination of the stepwise procedure. The output from step 51 is presented in Figure 5.7. The F statistic for the equation

```
Step51   Variable C417 Entered      R-square = 0.98271106    C(p) =620.60971646

              DF        Sum of Squares      Mean Square        F     Prob>F

Regression    35      380696.59484958    10877.04556713    1195.27   0.0001
Error        736        6697.63419169        9.10004646
Total        771      387394.22904127
```

Variable	Parameter Estimate	Standard Error	Type II Sum of Squares	F	Prob>F
INTERCEP	-594345.2736046	91891.46554201	380.68948408	41.83	0.0001
TIME	85.16028767	13.19794466	378.88310781	41.64	0.0001
TIME2	-0.00304976	0.00047389	376.89535343	41.42	0.0001
C2	0.00000705	0.00000156	185.81715392	20.42	0.0001
C112	-0.00004084	0.00000515	571.27614540	62.78	0.0001
C155	0.00015513	0.00001037	2037.11672643	223.86	0.0001
C201	-0.00096016	0.00007143	1644.24198065	180.69	0.0001
C207	0.00083574	0.00006906	1332.69019114	146.45	0.0001
C277	0.00017794	0.00002885	346.11365950	38.03	0.0001
C298	-0.00042152	0.00005698	497.99543284	54.72	0.0001
C318	0.00033950	0.00004671	480.70158212	52.82	0.0001
C355	-0.00017949	0.00002965	333.45197456	36.64	0.0001
C386	0.00018658	0.00003731	227.55761271	25.01	0.0001
C417	-0.00031089	0.00006653	198.71334101	21.84	0.0001
C437	0.00060530	0.00009763	349.80505772	38.44	0.0001
C457	-0.00069903	0.00009108	536.00642579	58.90	0.0001
C488	0.00090795	0.00016413	278.48195263	30.60	0.0001
C495	-0.00067700	0.00014622	195.08434739	21.44	0.0001
C537	0.00065893	0.00008802	510.01073743	56.04	0.0001
C552	-0.00153402	0.00015416	901.09637663	99.02	0.0001
C572	0.00217681	0.00023161	803.82930632	88.33	0.0001
C587	-0.00200982	0.00029131	433.14810388	47.60	0.0001
C611	0.01476368	0.00218013	417.32065354	45.86	0.0001
C615	-0.02441286	0.00347958	447.94889549	49.22	0.0001
C623	0.02639754	0.00397860	400.59839117	44.02	0.0001
C626	-0.01667138	0.00268263	351.45197541	38.62	0.0001
C648	0.00146880	0.00026593	277.60699761	30.51	0.0001
C669	-0.00269366	0.00038753	439.66595175	48.31	0.0001
C680	0.00353795	0.00058386	334.14410126	36.72	0.0001
C693	-0.00288357	0.00063787	185.97089899	20.44	0.0001
C710	0.03247751	0.00515891	360.65611001	39.63	0.0001
C712	-0.03414331	0.00516210	398.10872625	43.75	0.0001
C728	0.00459249	0.00050333	757.60133245	83.25	0.0001
C752	-0.14468196	0.01961668	495.01851683	54.40	0.0001
C753	0.15648446	0.02153513	480.49751418	52.80	0.0001
C763	-0.02980794	0.00578664	241.46539244	26.53	0.0001

```
Bounds on condition number:    9.059E9,    1.256E12
```

Figure 5.7. Stepwise Regression Output for Step 51

as a whole is down somewhat from its 2399.97 value in step 7 and 1777.33 value in step 19, but it is still quite respectable at 1195.27. Meanwhile the R-squared value has reached a value over .98. Moreover, the 36 regression coefficients are all highly statistically significant

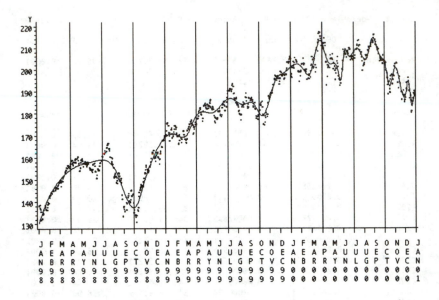

Figure 5.8. Graph of Actual/Predicted CREF Stock Values at Step 51

with *p* values less than .0001. Again notice that the tendency for the coefficients to alternate in sign is still quite strong.

Figure 5.8 shows the graphical results for step 51. For the short-term investor, this provides a much more detailed analysis of the market behavior of the CREF Stock unit values. At least historically you can see where moving from CREF Stock to cash or a cash equivalent, such as the CREF Money Market account, would have been a good move. The additional volatility captured by step 51 is particularly evident in the year 2000, where most of the sharp drops and rebounds have been picked up quite well. From the point of view of representing past performance, the model generally, and step 51, in particular, works quite well.

Spline Regression Forecasting

Although the historical results from our curve-fitting exercise look quite good, we might also want to know about the possible future performance of the CREF Stock. Although poring over graphs of past performance, like rerunning clips from past football games, may be interesting, it does not, by itself, provide an adequate idea of what might be done to improve performance. Unfortunately, the answer to this involves quite sophistocated spline forecasting methods that use some highly complicated techniques that are beyond the scope of this book. However, we now present some graphical output from such efforts to give the reader some sense of what is possible and how our preliminary research in this area has worked out.

The in-sample data for this forecasting effort were from April 1, 1988 to the end of December 1998. The data from this period were used to estimate the parameters of a 90-day forecast model designed to predict the CREF Stock unit values 90 days in advance so you would have an opportunity to adjust your portfolio before any significant downturn or upturn. Figure 5.9 displays the results of projecting beyond the end of the sample data to the out-of-sample period from January 1, 1999 through December 31, 2000. The jagged-line forecast displays considerably more volatility than the data series itself. Consequently, it makes sense to mitigate this through some standard moving-average procedure. This step will be left for future research.

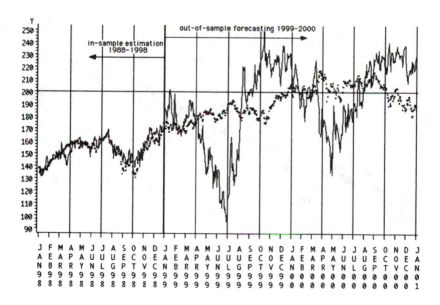

Figure 5.9. Graph of 90-Day Out-of-Sample Forecast of CREF Stock Unit Values

60

Finally, we used the data from 1988 through 1998 to estimate a
30-day spline forecasting model. We again projected our forecasts
throughout 1999 and 2000 to get a general sense of how well our
method might perform out-of-sample. Figure 5.10 presents a graph of
in-sample results for 1998 and out-of-sample forecasts for the 1999 to
2000 period.

In viewing this graph, we can immediately see that our 30-day forecasts stay closer to the actual 1999-2000 CREF Stock unit values
than in our 90-day forecast. This contrast clearly reveals the trade-off
between longer term forecasts and more accurate forecasts. However,
even the 30-day forecast is not entirely satisfactory, because there are
many points in time where the forecast would mislead us and result in
even greater losses than a simple buy-and-hold strategy. This is especially true in the Fall of 1999 and the Fall of 2000, where the forecast
is relatively more volatile.

Clearly, a lot more work is needed to develop good quality forecasts for mutual fund instruments such as the CREF Stock account.
Splines provide one of many possible tools for pursuing this objective,

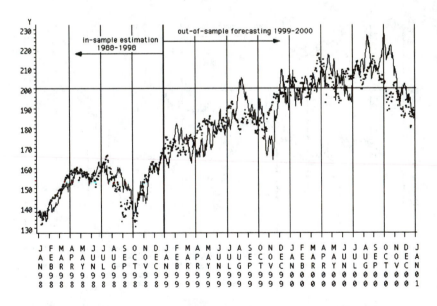

Figure 5.10. Graph of 30-Day Out-of-Sample Forecast of CREF Stock Unit
Values

but we think it is a promising one. Of course, even the limited methods developed here might be useful for short-term forecasting of less volatile data series such as population census counts or automobile sales.

6. SUMMARY AND CONCLUSIONS

We have attempted to provide the reader with an understanding of spline regression models. Spline regression has been seen as an extension of or a restricted version of interrupted regression and polynomial regression rather than simply as an alternative to these methods. By citing references from the literature and providing detailed research applications, we have attempted to demonstrate the appropriateness and the usefulness of spline methods in practical, social science research.

More specifically, although Chapter 1 pointed to a variety of potential uses for spline regression, it focused primarily upon the study of political party identification among voters in the 1984 U.S. Presidential elections by Allsop and Weisburg (1988). They identified four phases of the election campaign and estimated the four regression lines subject to three corresponding spline knot restrictions. Although they used piecewise linear splines, we pointed out that they could have used quadratic or cubic splines with the same number of parameters, but with increased flexibility and increased smoothness. We did not have their data, so we did not get to try out these alternative specifications.

Chapter 2 compared splines with interrupted regression as exemplified in the work of Lewis-Beck (1986) and McDowell et al. (1980). Splines were introduced as dummy variables models with one or more smoothing restriction using the adjustment approach introduced by Smith (1979). Using simulated data on a politician's performance approval ratings, spline regression was presented as an extension or restricted version of interrupted regression, using methods explained by Pindyck and Rubinfeld (1998), and then compared to polynomial regression. A key aspect of this spline example was explaining how to transform the spline parameters into the corresponding traditional regression coefficients (i.e., intercepts and slopes).

Chapter 3 demonstrated the estimation of spline knots with known locations in a research attempt to determine if the control of the

White House by Democrats or Republicans had an effect on interest rates for 6-month commercial bonds. Using the 11 times since 1890 when the White House switched hands, we tested to see whether interest rates went up or down more during Republican administrations than during Democratic administrations. Surprisingly enough, we discovered that although interest rates tend to fall under both Republican and Democratic administrations, they actually tend to fall more under Democrates. In the comparison of linear, quadratic, and higher order splines, including hybrid splines, we considered the adjusted R-squared, the F statistic, the t statistics, a measure of multicollinearity, and the Durbin–Watson test for first-order autocorrelation. We concluded that there was no "one size fits all" solution to the problem of selecting the most desirable model, but rather that the purpose of the analysis was key to determining how much weight to give each factor.

Chapter 4 took research with splines one step further by demonstrating how to estimate the location of spline knots rather than assuming their location a priori. Although this made things more interesting, it did so at the cost of requiring the use of nonlinear least squares regression. The research issue (taken from the sociology of religion) concerned the relationship between a measure of a person's commitment to religion and his or her age in years. The original spline knot locations of 35, 55, and 75 years of age were transformed to approximately 38, 45, and 71, respectively, by the nonlinear least squares estimation procedure. The Wald test and some common-sense intuition were used to select the optimal model from linear and quadratic candidates.

Finally, Chapter 5 dealt with the problem of determining the number of spline knots, their polynomial power (linear, squared, cubic, etc.), and their locations. Using least squares regression, a stepwise procedure selected from among a large number of potential knot locations, adding one knot at a time according to its statistical significance. The research example used here was the CREF Stock value from the TIAA–CREF retirement system. Different degrees of smoothing were used for long-, medium-, and short-term investing. Both 30- and 90-day forecasting were demonstrated with rather limited success for the CREF Stock value.

The examples provided hopefully have given the reader an understanding of when spline regression models are appropriate, how such models are formulated and estimated, and how to choose from among alternative spline regression models.

APPENDIX

SAS® Program to Calculate Standard Error[2]

```
DATA ONE; *DEMOCRATIC VS. REPUBLICAN EFFECT ON INTEREST RATES;
  INPUT INTEREST @@; N+1; YEAR = 1889+N;
  IF YEAR > 1888 THEN REP1 = 1; ELSE REP1 = 0; RYEAR1 = REP1*(YEAR-1888);
  IF YEAR > 1892 THEN DEM1 = 1; ELSE DEM1 = 0; DYEAR1 = DEM1*(YEAR-1892);
  IF YEAR > 1896 THEN REP2 = 1; ELSE REP2 = 0; RYEAR2 = REP2*(YEAR-1896);
  IF YEAR > 1912 THEN DEM2 = 1; ELSE DEM2 = 0; DYEAR2 = DEM2*(YEAR-1912);
  IF YEAR > 1920 THEN REP3 = 1; ELSE REP3 = 0; RYEAR3 = REP3*(YEAR-1920);
  IF YEAR > 1932 THEN DEM3 = 1; ELSE DEM3 = 0; DYEAR3 = DEM3*(YEAR-1932);
  IF YEAR > 1952 THEN REP4 = 1; ELSE REP4 = 0; RYEAR4 = REP4*(YEAR-1952);
  IF YEAR > 1960 THEN DEM4 = 1; ELSE DEM4 = 0; DYEAR4 = DEM4*(YEAR-1960);
  IF YEAR > 1968 THEN REP5 = 1; ELSE REP5 = 0; RYEAR5 = REP5*(YEAR-1968);
  IF YEAR > 1976 THEN DEM5 = 1; ELSE DEM5 = 0; DYEAR5 = DEM5*(YEAR-1976);
  IF YEAR > 1980 THEN REP6 = 1; ELSE REP6 = 0; RYEAR6 = REP6*(YEAR-1980);
  IF YEAR > 1992 THEN DEM6 = 1; ELSE DEM6 = 0; DYEAR6 = DEM6*(YEAR-1992);
  CARDS;
  6.91 6.48 5.40 7.64 5.22 5.80 7.02 4.72 5.34 5.50 5.71 5.40 5.81 6.16
  5.14 5.18 6.25 6.66 5.00 4.67 5.72 4.75 5.41 6.20 5.47 4.01 3.84 5.07
  6.02 5.37 7.50 6.62 4.52 5.07 3.98 4.02 4.34 4.11 4.85 5.85 3.59 2.64
  2.73 1.73 1.02 0.76 0.75 0.94 0.81 0.59 0.56 0.53 0.66 0.69 0.73 0.75
  0.81 1.03 1.44 1.49 1.45 2.16 2.33 2.52 1.58 2.18 3.31 3.81 2.46 3.97
  3.85 2.97 3.26 3.55 3.97 4.38 5.55 5.10 5.90 7.83 7.71 5.11 4.73 8.15
  9.84 6.32 5.34 5.61 7.99 10.91 12.29 14.76 11.89 8.89 10.16 8.01 6.39
  6.85 7.68 8.80 7.95 5.85 3.80 3.30 4.93 5.93 5.42 5.51 5.34 5.18
  ;
PROC REG OUTEST = BETAS COVOUT;
MODEL INTEREST = RYEAR1-RYEAR6 DYEAR1-DYEAR6 / P DW; OUTPUT
OUT = NEWDATA P = PINTRATE;
data coeff; set betas; if _TYPE_ = 'PARMS'; keep RYEAR1-RYEAR6
DYEAR1-DYEAR6;

data COVD; set betas; if _TYPE_ = 'COV'; n+1; if 2 le n le 13;
keep RYEAR1-RYEAR6 DYEAR1-DYEAR6;
PROC IML; use coeff; read all into bt; b = bt`;
LT1 = J(12,12,1); DO i = 1 to 12; do j = 1 to 12; if i<j then
LT1[i,j] = 0; end; end;
d = LT1*b; use COVD; read all into COVD;
AREP = {3 16 12 8 8 12}/59; ADEM = {4 8 20 8 4 7}/51; AREP = -1*AREP;
A = AREP||ADEM;
ddiff = A*d;   ACOVA = A*COVD*A`;   reverse = vecdiag(diag(d*A));
```

```
WALD = ddiff` *inv(ACOVA)*ddiff; tstat = sqrt(WALD);
tstatt = ddiff/sqrt(ACOVA);
print b     d , ddiff , A , COVD , WALD, tstat tstatt reverse;
```

NOTES

1. Although assumptions are often stated concerning the error term, for practical purposes these assumptions are more appropriately expressed in terms of the behavior of the conditional distribution of the dependent variable.

2. SAS is a registered trademark in the United States and other countries of SAS Institute, Inc., of Cary, NC. ® indicates U.S. registration.

3. Statistically this is not a problem because we are assuming that the dependent variables Y_1 through Y_{110} are jointly normally distributed (and, therefore, the regression error terms are also jointly normally distributed). Whereas the regression coefficient estimators (the bs) are linear combinations of the Ys, then the bs also must be jointly normally distributed, which is standard in regression analysis. Finally, any linear combination of the bs will itself be normally distributed (because any linear combination of jointly normally distributed random variables must itself be normally distributed). Whereas the true population standard errors are unknown and have to be estimated from the sample data, we will easily obtain a Student's t test statistic for this problem because we are testing a single linear restriction on a linear model.

REFERENCES

ALLSOP, D., and WEISBERG, H. F. (1988). Measuring change in party identification in an election campaign. *American Journal of Political Science, 32*(4), 996–1017.

BUSE, A., and LIM, L. (1977). Cubic splines as a special case of restricted least squares. *Journal of the American Statistical Association 72*, 64–68.

CARROLL, R. J. (2000). *Nonparametric regression in longitudinal models: Locality of kernel and spline methods.* Paper presented to the Department of Statistics, Purdue University, November 30.

GREENE, W. H. (2000). *Econometric analysis.* Upper Saddle River, NJ: Prentice–Hall.

KANBUR, S. M. R. (1983). Labor supply under uncertainty with piecewise linear tax regimes. *Economica, 5*(200), 379–394.

LEEGE, D. C., and KELLSTEDT, L. A. (1993). *Rediscovering the religious factor in American politics.* Armonk, NY: M.E. Sharpe.

LEEGE, D. C., KELLSTEDT, L. A., and WALD, K. D. (1990). *Religion and politics: A report on measures of religiosity in the 1989 NES pilot study.* Paper presented at the annual meeting of the Midwest Political Science Association, Chicago.

LEWIS-BECK, M. S. (1986). Interrupted time series. In W. O. Berry and M. S. Lewis-Beck (Eds.), *New tools for social scientists: Advances and applications.* Newbury Park, CA: Sage.

MARSH, L. C. (1983). On estimating spline regressions. *Proceedings of SAS® Users Group International, 8*, 723–728.

MARSH, L. C. (1986). Estimating the number and location of knots in spline regressions. *Journal of Applied Business Research, 3*, 60–70.

MARSH, L. C., MAUDGAL, M., and RAMAN, J. (1990). Alternative methods of estimating piecewise linear and higher order regression models using SAS® software. *Proceedings of SAS® Users Group International, 15*, 523–527.

MARSH, L. C., McGLYNN, M., and CHAKRABORTY, D. (1994). Interpreting complex nonlinear models. *Proceedings of SAS® User's Group International, 19*, 1185–1189.

MARSH, L. C., and SINDONE, A. B. (1991). A calibration technique for estimating the effect of location on the values of residential properties. *The Property Tax Journal, 10*(2), 261–276.

McDOWALL, D., McCLEARY, R., MEIDINGER, E. E., and HAY, R. A. (1980). *Interrupted time series analysis.* Newbury Park, CA: Sage.

McNEIL, D. R., TRUSSELL, T. J., and TURNER, J. C. (1977). Spline interpolation of demographic data. *Demography, 14*(2), 245–252.

PINDYCK, R. S., and RUBINFELD, D. L. (1998). *Econometric models and economic forecasts,* (4th ed.) New York: Irwin/McGraw-Hill.

POIRIER, D. J. (1973). Piecewise regression using cubic splines. *Journal of the American Statistical Association, 68*, 515–524.

SMITH, P. L. (1979). Splines as a useful and convenient statistical tool. *The American Statistician, 33*(2), 57–62.

SPEYRER, J. F., and RAGAS, W. R. (1991). Housing prices and flood risk: An examination using spline regressions. *Journal of Real Estate Finance and Economics, 4*(4), 395–407.

STRAWCZYNSKI, M. (1998). Social insurance and the optimal piecewise linear income tax. *Journal of Public Economics, 63*(3), 371–388.

SUITS, D. B., MASON, A., and CHAN, L. (1978). Spline functions fitted by standard regression methods. *Review of Economics and Statistics, 60*, 132–139.

ABOUT THE AUTHORS

LAWRENCE C. MARSH served as Director of Graduate Studies at the University of Notre Dame for 13 years and as a liaison with the Laboratory for Social Research at Notre Dame. He is cofounder of and the meetings coordinator for the Midwest Econometrics Group. He has authored over 75 professional publications in a wide variety of journals and books, and has presented papers over 125 times at professional conferences, seminars, and workshops outside of Notre Dame. At Notre Dame, he has given over 2,000 lectures on statistics and econometrics at the graduate and undergraduate levels, and has served on 79 Ph.D. dissertation committees. He received his Ph.D. from Michigan State University.

DAVID R. CORMIER is a Staff Associate in the Division of Labor Studies at Indiana University, Kokomo. His current research is on the effects of deindustrialization and U.S. trade policy on labor market outcomes, and the impact of these trends on income inequality and the growth of working poor households. He teaches in the Indiana University credit program in labor studies and labor education in the state. He worked for nearly 20 years as a labor organizer, staff representative, and officer in the labor movement. He has his Ph.D. in labor economics from the University of Notre Dame.